RESEARCH AND THE SOCIAL WORK PICTURE

Ian Shaw

First published in Great Britain in 2018 by

Policy Press
University of Bristol
1-9 Old Park Hill
Bristol
BS2 8BB
UK
t: +44 (0)117 954 5940
pp-info@bristol.ac.uk
www.policypress.co.uk

North America office:
Policy Press
c/o The University of Chicago Press
1427 East 60th Street
Chicago, IL 60637, USA
t: +1 773 702 7700
f: +1 773-702-9756
sales@press.uchicago.edu
www.press.uchicago.edu

British Library Cataloguing in Publication Data
A catalogue record for this book is available from the British Library

Library of Congress Cataloging-in-Publication Data
A catalog record for this book has been requested

ISBN 978-1-4473-3889-5 hardcover
ISBN 978-1-4473-3892-5 ePub
ISBN 978-1-4473-3893-2 Mobi
ISBN 978-1-4473-3891-8 epdf

Cover design by Policy Press
Front cover image: istock
Printed and bound in Great Britain by CPI Group (UK) Ltd, Croydon, CR0 4YY
Policy Press uses environmentally responsible print partners

Research in social work

Series editors:
Ian Shaw, National University of Singapore, Singapore and
John Gal, Hebrew University of Jerusalem, Israel

The *Research in Social Work* series, published with the European Social Work Research Association, examines current, progressive and innovative research on social work in Europe. A leading collection for social work academics, researchers and practitioners, it makes a unique contribution to this international field.

The series editors invite proposals for books drawing on original and cutting-edge research and which aim to influence social work academia and practice. They can be contacted through either the office of the European Social Work (info@eswra.org) or Policy Press (pp-info@bristol.ac.uk).

Forthcoming titles in the series:

Jobling, H. (2019) *Power and control in social work: An ethnographic account of mental health practice*

Devlieghere, J. (2019) *Digital technologies and social work: Opportunities and illusions*

Klammer, U., Leiber, S. and Leitner, S. (2019) *Social work and the making of social policy*

Nygren, L., Oltedal, S. and White, S. (2019) *International social work with families: Comparing contexts and complexities in Europe, Latin America and Australia*

European Social Work Research Association

Dedication

I acknowledge those audiences of practitioners, students and faculty in Europe, Asia and the US who have been forbearing, interested and responsive enough to allow me a hearing, and dedicate this book to them.

Contents

List of figures and tables

Introduction

The purpose of this book is to provide social work students at different levels and in different countries with a detailed sketch of how research finds a place in the wider social work picture. While authors (too) often claim a distinctiveness for their writing, I am here aiming to deal with questions that in their detail and also their relation to one another are rarely covered in the social work literature.

I have endeavoured to provide an accessible entry point for thinking hard about social work in general and research in particular. In other parts of my writing I have tried to work through these issues to more scholarly audiences, but here I write for students and practitioners. As much of the book draws on presentations to just such audiences, the level and tone of the book will, I hope, be ensured. My aim is to engage social work students in questions and issues in a form that will make for a professional community that is thoughtful, critical and committed, yet also – I dare to say – modest.

I have tried to make clear what this book does not set out to provide. It is not a research methods book at any level. Nor is it solely about research, but rather about research as part of a larger picture. I anticipate that one feature of the book that will quickly be noticed is the number of quotations from interviews with scientists in what we generally regard as the mainstream sciences. This is quite intentional, and reflects the conviction that social work has too easily fenced itself off from other disciplines.

I do not claim to be innovative in these pages. Almost all of the issues tackled are those that I have endeavoured to think and write about over the past decade. But rather than attempt to re-lay scholarly foundations, my concern in these pages is to try something equally demanding and communicate in an accessible and stimulating way the superstructures of practice supported by such foundations.

The approach and layout of the book are rather different from most texts. It may help to say that throughout I move between accessible ways of thinking hard and opportunities and exercises that progressively support the reader in making sense of the material in their day-to-day course programmes, practice placements and research. I have done this in two ways – by the inclusion of short-task boxes and by the presence, where appropriate, of closing sections on 'making practical sense' of the chapter material. I also have included some boxed material where it seems useful to spell out some examples in more concrete detail.

The short-task boxes are embedded, woven into the chapters. This is one of the more innovative features of the book. The reason for doing so is to facilitate reflection and development in the here and now as the book is read. Rather than read through a whole chapter, the intention is for readers to pause mid-current and bring their own thoughts and experience to bear. Sometimes this will involve moving away from the book. For example, the very first such box presents a task about the much-used but not well thought-through idea that good research and science may depend on 'serendipity'. Task Box 1.1 suggests: 'Readers undertaking dissertation or thesis work or early career research might ask a senior research figure whose work they respect if s/he puts any of their "success" down to serendipity.' Tasks such as this may be undertaken as 'solo' mini-projects or as part of a group activity or seminar. Often they can be undertaken at different levels.

While some of these tasks encourage associated reading (Task Box 2.1, for instance, urges the value of actually reading Thomas Kuhn's ground-breaking book *The structure of scientific revolutions*), I have resisted the familiar practice of including further reading for each chapter. This is partly because I confess from experience that I rarely, if ever, pursue such well-intended advice, and partly because the end references give enough scope for interested readers to see where I am coming from – and where they may choose to go.

In addition, reflection on the practice implications of the discussion is prompted in some chapters by the inclusion of closing sections on 'making practical sense'. In speaking about these issues from country to country, I have been obliged to facilitate just such opportunities, often when audiences have been working through English as a second language. As with the approach to language in the book as a whole, I try to open up what we might mean when we talk about something being 'practical', and, if the reader is especially interested in this question, Chapter Three is almost wholly devoted to that theme.

Finally, the reader may find it useful to read the opening of Chapter One where the structure of the book is outlined, and different possible paths through the material are suggested. I have written with various audiences in mind, and this is reflected in the options for route setting. But the book is a jigsaw, and the relation of research to the wider social work picture will remain incomplete if I tempt the reader to pick and choose.

What do I hope for as a result of writing this book? To embolden a particular kind of scepticism while at the same time providing the ground work for social workers becoming more thoughtfully practical – and practically thoughtful.

ONE

What is social work research?

Through this chapter, we will set out what seems feasible by way of describing the nature of social work and its linked research. We will then step back to say that, if we are to have a clear sense of what 'research' means, both in general and in our own field, we need to think what 'science' means. This will include a brief consideration of the relationship between 'science' and 'art.' Following from that, we will ask the curious question – curious because it seems strange but also because it encourages curiosity – of whether successful, interesting, or worthwhile research depends at all on serendipity. We will then ask whether research in social work is or ought to be marked by particular values. In closing, we will ask in what sense social work research is a field with a distinctive identity that demarcates it from other fields.

Rather than offer up a catalogue of ready-reference definitions of 'science', 'research', 'social work' and so on, this first chapter is framed around a very selective set of questions, with the hope that they will provide suspension lines that, unlike the unfortunate Millennium Bridge in London, will not oscillate unduly. In doing so, we will encounter at least as many questions as we answer. For the most part, these will be left where they lie and taken up in later chapters of the book. Some of this chapter and parts of Chapter Two are among the slightly more demanding parts of the book. As most of the chapters can be read as free-standing pieces, these opening chapters could be held back until later in the book. Chapters One, Two and Eight bookend the writing, and could be read together. Chapters One and Two are about the nature and purpose of social work research. The distinction is not a cut-and-dried one. When we come to talk about the *nature* of social work or research we often find ourselves answering by saying what its *purpose* is. Take, for example, the opening mission statement of the European Social Work Research Association:[1]

---

[1]   www.eswra.org/bylaws.html (accessed 28 February 2017).

> The European Social Work Research Association takes forward the development, practice and utilization of social work research, to enhance knowledge about individual and social problems, and promote just and equitable societies.

The Society for Social Work and Research,[2] also headlines the purposes of research:

> The Society for Social Work and Research advances, disseminates, and translates research that addresses issues of social work practice and policy and promotes a diverse, just, and equitable society.

Social work

It would be reasonable to expect a book on social work research to say something about what counts as 'social work' in this context. This is treacherous territory. Each reader has their own sense of national history of how social work came to be, and of how this shifted from one period to another. It makes sense, for example, for those in former USSR countries and in parts of Asia to distinguish the history of social work as marked by 'before' and 'after' characteristics. But speaking in general, for those who write about professions and occupations it has been customary to start with the functions and attributes of professions. Abbott argues that these were really arguments about the structure rather than the functions of professions – 'something was a profession if it had a certain structure' (Abbott, 1995, p 547). This led to a theory of social work as the profession of interstitiality – mediating between all the others. Social work is about brokering – 'about boundaries: boundaries between institutions, boundaries between professions' (Abbott, 1995, p 549). This is a view of social work that many social workers embrace. An example of this approach is presented by Smale and colleagues (2000), who suggested that social care organisations need to go beyond operating as aid agencies focusing on the needs of individuals, and should increase their development capacity by working with other agencies and citizens to make communities more supportive and inclusive for vulnerable and excluded people.

But the problem is that social workers – indeed professionals in general – are not spending their time doing what the (idealistic) theory suggests. For example, much of the recent criticism of the advent of

[2]   http://secure.sswr.org/about-sswr/mission-statement (accessed 28 February 2017).

electronic assessment and recording systems in social work has behind it the remains of this idealistic notion of what social work is and ought to be about. Indeed, there is much in social work that we tend to be routinely romantic about or routinely cynical (Carey, 2014).

There is another problem about having such a theory about social work. Professionals – social workers and others – spend much time trying to colonise the turf of others, which suggests that what counts as the territory of a given profession is more a matter of how much professional land can be held, rather than something that belongs by its nature to this or that profession.

Finally, as part of my defence that I should not say too much about what social work is, the history of social work is often told in part as reflecting an emphasis on rationalisation and 'scientific' knowledge as its foundation. In the US, there has been much talk of what are called 'grand challenges' and social work as a science (see, for example, Brekke, 2012). This tactic 'works' to some extent within the profession – in the sense that enough people accept it as important to make the focus worth sustaining. But outside social work it matters not a lot. To the public, the central legitimacy of social work is linked not to science but to altruism. Social work has retained a public image based on a character trait – something unusual for a profession, though shared to some degree with nursing. This is reinforced by social work's connection in the public eye with people who citizens often fear – the mentally ill, the criminal and the poor. This perception is further reinforced by the low salaries associated with social work.

But altruism comes at a price, as social work is also associated with controversial groups such as child abusers, school refusal children and so on – the 'difficult and despised', as Abbott calls them (1995, p 562). Also the profession, in the UK at least, does not have many powerful friends – for example, bishops, university professors, social elites, or philanthropists.

Social work research

A relatively rare example of openly defining social work research is the following, from the International Federation of Social Workers (IFSW) and International Association of Schools of Social Work (IASSW):

> Social work bases its methodology on a systematic body of evidence-based knowledge derived from research and policy evaluation, including local and indigenous knowledge specific to its context. (IFSW/IASSW, 2007, p 6)

Social work includes:

> Knowledge of social work research and skills in the use of
> research methods, including ethical use of relevant research
> paradigms, and critical appreciation of the use of research
> and the different sources of knowledge about social work
> practice. (IFSW/IASSW, 2007, p 21)

Two observations can be made about these IFSW/IASSW statements.
First, the statements are fairly cross-cultural. For example, knowledge
is said rather uncontroversially to 'include' local and indigenous
knowledge, rather than to consist entirely in such knowledge. The
appeal to 'systematic' and 'evidence-based' knowledge alike suggests
a foundational role for mainstream science models. This suggests that
the main international groupings of social workers and social work
academics accept that these activities carry a large degree of common
ground across cultures and nations. Second, the statements seem to have
an aspirational dimension (is social work *actually* based on systematic
knowledge?) and so risk confusing the descriptive and the normative,
or taking the form of staking territorial claims.

It may be helpful to distinguish *fields* of research and research *problems*.
By a 'field', I have in mind categories such as:

- adult offenders/victims – a category in terms of service users or
  carers;
- people as members of communities – a category in terms of citizen
  populations;
- social work practitioners and managers – a category in terms of
  professional or policy communities.

By a 'problem', I refer to examples such as:

- understand/explain issues related equality, diversity, poverty and
  social exclusion;
- understand/develop/assess/evaluate social work practices, methods,
  or interventions;
- understand/promote learning and teaching about social work or
  related professions.

But these may not be universal, or at least they will be afforded different
weight from one part of the world to another. So I would say that
social work research is identifiable through a set of features, none of

which exclusively or exhaustively characterises it, but which can be seen to typify its scope and character as follows:

- The use of a broad range of research methods and an acceptance of different linkages between research method and research questions in the contexts, practices and domains of social work research.
- An underpinning quest for both usefulness *and* theoretical contributions so that research is not categorised as only 'pure' or 'applied'.
- A pervasive concern with social inclusion, justice and change.
- Work with stakeholders in different aspects of the research process, recognising the complex power relationships involved.

While this may not gain general agreement, my position is that we will not expect or require each particular research project to be marked by a strong emphasis on all four hallmarks.

A further distinction is important. In speaking of social work and of research, it is helpful to discriminate between the following:

- Social work research as empirically apparent. Kirk and Reid (2002) stressed the need for treating questions of research empirically. This applies to understanding epistemologies adopted by social workers as well as acknowledging that '[t]he bottom line for research utilization is what actually happens in the field among practitioners' (Kirk and Reid, 2002, p 194). We will think about social work research in this way in Chapter Four, by looking at what research actually finds its way into social work journals.
- Social work research as theoretical discourse. Much of this chapter is about exactly this question.
- Social work research as social and moral practice/s. This often comes into focus when researchers talk about research ethics. However, this often becomes formalised into a process of satisfying procedures laid down by systems of committees. It is more helpful to think of ethics as a dimension present through the whole process of research, and not one that can be put to bed through an initial committee process (Shaw, 2008). We will not have much to say about research ethics in this procedural sense, but in the final chapter we do bring together the broader question of what constitutes good research.

Being 'scientific' and doing 'science'

While there is a huge social work literature on 'research', there is very little on 'science', and what does exist often adopts the term science as a way of bolstering the standing of research or practice through expressions such as 'scientific practice'. This has especially been the case in the US. This is probably one reason why there have been few enthusiastic claims for social work as science in countries where scientific, evidence-based, or empirical forms of practice have been mistrusted. This is unfortunate.

While for some people – especially in the US, but also elsewhere – science and research are seen as ways of reducing uncertainty, I have found that often they *increase* uncertainty, and in so doing produce a helpful scepticism and doubt. The point was put to Foucault as a criticism, in relation to his book on punishment and prisons:

> If one talks to social workers in the prisons, one finds that the arrival of *Discipline and Punish* had an absolutely sterilizing, or rather anaesthetizing effect on them, because they felt your critique had an implacable logic which left them no possible room for initiative. (Foucault, 1991b, p 82)

He replied as follows:

> I'm not so sure what's been said over the last fifteen years has been quite so – how shall I put it? – demobilizing.... If the social workers you are talking about don't know which way to turn, this just goes to show that they're looking, and hence are not anaesthetized or sterilized at all – on the contrary. And it's because of the need not to tie them down or immobilize them that there can be no question for me of trying to tell 'what is to be done'. If the questions posed by the social workers you spoke of are going to assume their full amplitude, the most important thing is not to bury them under the weight of prescriptive, prophetic discourse. (Foucault, 1991b, p 84)

Is social work a science? I believe for various reasons that will surface throughout the book that this is an unhelpful question expressed in this way. It may be helpful to some degree to say that social work is a science-based occupation. But this is some way from saying that social work as such is a science. In general, I bring a view about science that in some but not all ways is like that of Weber. Science, he insisted in the gendered language almost universal at the time he was speaking (1919), demands a 'strange intoxication'. 'Without this passion ... you have no calling for science and you should do something else. For nothing is worthy of a man unless he can pursue it with passionate devotion' (Weber, 1948 [1919], p 135). As Medawar (1984, p 9) later expressed it, 'to be good at science one must want to be – and must feel a first stirring of that sense of disquiet at lack of comprehension that is one of a scientist's few distinguishing marks'. That entails 'power of application and [a] kind of fortitude' (1984, p 10). This reminds me of a remark attributed to Isaac Newton and the story of how, when asked how he had arrived at the theory of gravity, he replied, not by seeing an apple fall, but 'by thinking about it all the time'.

Science and art

Writing long ago, the sociologist MacIver was quite straight: 'The relation of sociology to social work is that of a science to an art' (MacIver, 1931, p 1). He goes on to aver that 'If we fail to recognize the significant difference ... we shall cherish false hopes and refuse true aids, whether as scientists or artists' (1931, p 1). Without wishing to rubbish what MacIver says, we should destabilise his assurance that the difference is cut and dried.

It is not new to think of social work as art, although a check of the use of 'art' in social work literature will show that, with some exceptions, 'references to social work as "art" usually mean social work as skill' (Timms, 1968, p 74). Timms left us one of the most penetrating discussions of the question that long predates the recent interweaving of the humanities and the social sciences (Timms, 1968) and England (1986) devoted a whole book to the subject. Adrienne Chambon (2008) helpfully flags up an article by Norman Denzin written expressly for a social work audience (Denzin, 2002) where he spoke of bringing social work closer to the arts via a 'poetics of social work'. She also foregrounds the memory of Howard Goldstein, who was 'the most adamant social work scholar' who 'repeatedly clamoured for an explicit convergence between social work, the humanities, and the arts' (Chambon, 2008, p 592). Chambon is surely right to mention an exhibit of stitching wedding dresses in rural Canada as a way of telling through material means of a woman's world and a mother–daughter relationship. Through examples she urges the case that the artist provides 'a way of grasping at something not yet named.

A "skin sense" of uncertainties at the edge of an experience that is still unworded' (2008, p 595).

Should we think this is true only for interpretive approaches to research, we should hear a theoretical chemist (Roald Hoffmann) and a particle physicist (Carlo Rubbia) recognise the affinities of science and art:

> I think poetry and a lot of science – theory building, the synthesis of molecules – are creation. They're acts of creation that are accomplished with craftsmanship, with an intensity, a concentration, a detachment, an economy of statement. All of these qualities matter in science and art. There's an aesthetic at work, there is a search for understanding. There is a valuation of complexity and simplicity, of symmetry and asymmetry. There is an act of communication, of speaking to others' (Hoffman, in Wolpert and Richards, 1997, p 23).

This is not, of course, to say they are the same. Hoffmann subsequently adds: 'One thing that's different is … that science is infinitely paraphraseable and art is not' (in Wolpert and Richards, 1997, p 23). Rubbia says of the scientific enterprise:

> [W]e are essentially driven not by … the success, but by a sort of passion, namely the desire of understanding better, to possess, if you like, a bigger part of the truth. Hence science, for me, is very close to art…. [I]n my view scientific discovery is an irrational act … and I see no difference between a scientist developing a marvellous discovery and an artist making a painting. (Rubbia, in Wolpert and Richards, 1997, p 197)

Is research success ever down to serendipity?

James Lovelock will go down in history for his idea of the Gaia principle, which postulates that the Earth functions as a self-regulating system. But less known is a reason he gave for having the freedom to do his work. Talking about why he went independent, he recalled his position working for the Medical Research Council in the UK. The problem was tenure – not that he didn't have it, but that he did. 'It made me feel that there were tramlines of inevitability going on all the way down to retirement and the grave. And this was a most stifling thing. It was dreadful' (Lovelock, in Wolpert and Richards, 1997, p 72). Leroy

Hood, a biotechnologist, has said something similar: 'At the heart of doing science ... is an independence, a realization that everyone has to have their own thing' (in Wolpert and Richards, 1997, p 39), even when working in a research team.

After completing a book on social work science, I found myself continuing to think about this problem, and also a related question of whether good research and science is explainable in terms of good luck or serendipity. It was brought into focus for me by Robert Merton and Elinor Barber's book, *The travels and adventures of serendipity* (Merton and Barber, 2004). Merton described serendipity in social science as 'an *unanticipated, anomalous and strategic* datum that becomes the occasion for developing a new theory or extending an existing theory' (Merton and Barber, 2004, p 236; emphasis in original). The term comes from a letter of an 18th-century man of letters, Horace Walpole:

> I once read a silly fairy-tale, called the Three Princes of Serendip: as their highnesses travelled, they were always making discoveries, by accidents and sagacity, of things which they were not in quest of: for instance, one of them discovered that a mule, blind of the right eye, had travelled the same road lately, because the grass was eaten only on the left side, where it was worse than on the right – now do you understand Serendipity? (Horace Walpole, 28 January 1754, in Merton and Barber, 2004, p 2)

In general, social work writers of widely varying epistemological positions have deployed the term, usually, but by no means always, to refer to the presence of chancy and positive moments in practice and research. However, few efforts have been made to elaborate its meaning and none to deal with the difficult questions it presents. The question is not playing a game. How discoveries are made is asked not for its own sake, but as a matter of practical strategy.

Task Box 1.1: Serendipity

Readers undertaking dissertation or thesis work or early career research might ask a senior research figure whose work they respect if s/he puts any of their 'success' down to serendipity.

Serendipity is 'that once rare but now adored word for the faculty of making pleasant, unexpected discoveries, inspired by the old name of that teardrop of a tropical island, Sri Lanka' (Hitchings, 2008, p 201). As early as 1938, Merton was observing that the telling of a scientific finding depends on creative storytelling, whereas scientific etiquette demands the 'retrospective streamlining of accounts of discovery', which underestimates the accidental, or contrarily the intrusion of human interest issues into accounts of discovery, which may exaggerate stress on the accidental. If so, this may have 'led to an inadequate understanding both of the nature of science and of the qualities of scientists' (Merton and Barber, 2004, p 159).

Most social work references are slight, or are used to bury or praise. Stephen Webb, for example, speaks of 'mere serendipity' when he remarks: 'We judge the situation and what is needed and this takes the successful action beyond mere serendipity' (Webb, 2006, p 220). Social work writers, when they refer to the term, often do so within a list of what are probably seen as related terms. Gomory, for example, refers to the word under a list of elements within clinical judgement including professional experience (good or bad), serendipity, personal whim, intuition and client choice (Gomory, 2001). Rodwell says that 'the interpretive perspective to research and practice in social work acknowledges that research and knowledge building are a mix of the rational, serendipitous and intuitive' (1998, p 16). By contrast with positivism, 'from the interpretive perspective the serendipitous and intuitive are not liabilities but opportunities in the effort to understand human phenomena' (Rodwell, 1998, p 16). However, she does not say what serendipity entails.

A definition is offered by Holesko and Thyer. 'Serendipitous information' is 'data that a researcher learns by chance during the course of a study that ends up being helpful to the study, although the researcher had not known that it would be when the study was designed' (Holesko and Thyer, 2011, p 115). A curious contrast to this can be found elsewhere, when Thyer tells a story about 'serendipity or the role of chance' – curious because he tells a story that presents a different idea from the definition he gave. Here he talks of serendipity as something that takes place independently of the study rather than within it:

> My own work as a clinician brought me into contact with clients who suffered from trichotillomania (TTM), or compulsive hair pulling. One evening I was having drinks and dinner at the home of one of my doctoral students,

Patrick Bordnick, who, serendipitously, had two cockatoos … as pets. As we consumed our adult beverages, we watched with amusement the antics of the birds walking about the room, preening themselves, climbing curtains, and so on. Pat began telling me about a behavioral problem called feather pecking disorder…. We began laughing at the apparent similarities between trichotillomania in humans and feather pecking disorder in birds. What began as a bibulous conversation subsequently led to a legitimate investigation of two literatures. (Thyer, 2009, p 479)

If 'useful discoveries may be made in unexpected ways, it will pay off to take this possibility into consideration'. For example, it may suggest that 'the absence of rigid control over the work that scientists do facilitates the discovery of important things by accident' (Merton and Barber, 2004, p 144). This has relevance to social work because it is an occupational status that carries a high degree of uncertainty *and* a high level of responsibility. Thus social workers, like the example of doctors that Merton and Barber employ, 'are often incapable of specifying the conditions under which certain kinds of therapy will succeed, and in such situations they may obtain positive or negative results without knowing why' (pp 154-5).

An illustration from direct practice may help. In one study, social workers generally took the view that, however experienced and wise a social worker may be, there remains an element of unpredictability near the heart of social work practice (Shaw and Shaw, 1997). At its simplest, the stance was reflected in the assumption of one social worker that 'there's always an element of good fortune in these things', and in the words of two other participants:

Whether it was because the time was right for her and I was just lucky that I connected, I don't know. I think it was just sheer luck. It's a bit like gambling and roulette, and every now and then you score the right number and you make a good connection with somebody. (in Shaw and Shaw, 1997)

I've been trying to help (the group) for three or four years. I don't know what happened. I was really dreading it, and I went in and I flew through it. I mean it was like flying, it was such a brilliant experience for me…. It was a one-off. (in Shaw and Shaw, 1997)

There was a commonly expressed belief that cases are capable of 'blowing up into a total nightmare', assuming that there are aspects of work beyond the control of even the seasoned practitioner: 'I don't feel I did the piece of work as well as I might have done, but having said that, there were elements in it that were totally out of my control' (in Shaw and Shaw, 1997)

Walpole's account raises the question of what is accident and what is sagacity. As Merton and Barber remark, 'a discovery is accidental if the object discovered is not being sought – but whether it is merely not being sought *at the time* of its discovery, or whether for true serendipity its existence should be unknown to, and even unsuspected by the discoverer, is not clear' (2004, p 187). Those who allow for serendipity and the accident have been vague on how to specify 'the auspicious conditions for accidental discoveries.... Making room for the crucial element of surprise is as difficult as preventing it' (Merton and Barber, 2004, p 187). The accidents we wish for have to be of a particular kind, and have positive implications for social work. And they must be capable of repetition.[3] 'Such accidents don't just grow on trees.' How then might serendipity – the discovery of unanticipated, anomalous and strategic data – happen in science? 'We need to concentrate on turning small happenings into big ideas and big ideas into local phenomena' and by 'big ideas' Atkinson means '*generic* ideas that transcend local, specific, contingent phenomena' (Atkinson, 2013, p 60). So how should we think of the ideal balance between planned and unplanned research or practice interventions?

We heard Merton and Barber suggesting that the absence of rigid control over the work that scientists do facilitates the discovery of important things by accident. This becomes a more considered argument later in their book through the idea that plans should be made but only of a general kind – 'planning in general with indefiniteness as to specific problems' (Merton and Baber, 2004, p 192). 'Compulsive tidiness' keeps the scientist from being open to fruitful surprises. This pushes to the fore questions of the ideal organisation of social work science, for example where resources should be concentrated. This will depend on whether we believe that best science is done by the

[3]   At the time of writing, there has been much discussion of what is referred to as the replication or reproducibility crisis. This refers to a methodological crisis in science in which scientists have found that the results of many scientific experiments are difficult or impossible to replicate on subsequent investigation, either by independent researchers or by the original researchers themselves. It has been discussed particularly in the fields of psychology and medicine where a number of efforts have been made to reinvestigate and repeat classic studies.

great scientists, by serendipitous scientists, or by 'anyone busy with science' (p. 207).

This discussion has obvious relevance for social work. Much programmatic research is carried out in research units and teams that undertake a succession of studies where the funding contracts leave little or no space for the kind of flexible lack of specificity that I believe Merton and Barber were right to value. As James Black, a Nobel-winning pharmacologist, confessed:

> The place of discipline in life is one which I've never really solved, because it is both a necessity and an impediment to the way I work. In other words, I have to be disciplined in my thinking in a sense, but at the same time it has to take place under circumstances where it isn't too focused. (in Wolpert and Richards, 1997, p 128)

Values and science

A question familiar from university days to even the noviciate social worker is about the relationship between values and science, and whether science should be value-free in some sense. For those of a certain generation, the default answer to this question, recalled from a distant past, is that it is not possible to infer what we *ought* to do from a statement about what *is*.[4]

It will help in unpacking this if we refer to the arguments of critical theory. 'Critical', you may have noticed, is a favourite word in social work. Critical theory is a catch-all term to include neo-Marxist science, some feminist positions, the work of Paolo Freire, and some forms of participatory inquiry. Critical inquiry focuses on the contradictions of practice. Hence the basic logic is preoccupied with 'particular forms of reasoning that give focus to scepticism towards social institutions' (Popkewitz, 1990, p 49).

Horkheimer, a founding figure in the critical theory field, speaking in the 1930s, distinguished *traditional* and *critical* theory. For critical theory, the current social situation influences scientific structures and not 'sheer logic alone' (Horkheimer, 2002, p 195). Theorising is not only 'an intrascienfic process but a social one as well' (p 196). By

---

[4]   This refers to how the 18th-century Scottish philosopher, David Hume, saw the difference between positive statements (about what is) and prescriptive or normative statements (about what ought to be). This position was, for him, associated with moral scepticism.

contrast, 'In traditional theoretical thinking, the genesis of particular objective facts, the practical application of the conceptual systems by which it grasps the facts, and the role of such systems in action, are all taken to be external to the theoretical thinking itself' (p 208). This finds expression in the separation of fact and value, knowledge and action. 'Traditional theory may take a number of things for granted: its positive role in a functioning society, an admittedly indirect and obscure relation to the satisfaction of general needs, and participation in the self-renewing life process. But all these exigencies ... are called into question in critical thought' (p 216). Hence, critical knowledge is never neutral. 'It is always for some particular subject' (Comstock, 1982, p 374). The production of knowledge is the production of values.

On the matter of value-free science in social work or any other field, many of the consequent questions can be seen by scanning a long-ago discussion by Madge. At one extreme, he says, 'is the stand taken by those who may be called naïve behaviourists, who are determined that all science is value-free' (Madge, 1953, p 14). For Madge, 'Freedom from value-judgment is an unreal imperative because it is unrealisable' (p 17). An alternative position is that the social scientist ought to have a standpoint on social issues and that without it the investigator would 'lapse into the random collection of pointless facts and will claim immunity from the need to organise these facts and to act upon them until some unattainable time when all the data are safely gathered in' (p 15). This implies a duty to choose a position within certain limits and in accord with values of society.

For others, objectivity is seen as something never attainable, yet acting as a 'regulatory ideal' – a stance I find rather attractive. This position is sometimes adopted by Christian philosophers of science. MacKay readily concedes that 'any idea that the practice of science can be value-neutral is nonsensical; our decisions whether, when and at what cost to lift the lid of Pandora's Box ... are as value-laden as human judgements can be. But for the working scientist ... the leap that he should on these grounds abandon his ideal of value-free knowledge as a 'myth' is a monstrous non-sequitur' (1987, p 14).

Regardless of the faith position of the social work researcher, Helm's (1987) conclusions about why an objective attitude is a good thing are of wider value to most epistemological starting points. The nearest he comes to defining an objective attitude is 'adopting the attitudes of impartiality, a willingness to have second thoughts, to consider alternative hypotheses, together with their associated practical techniques, such as careful measurement and the use of controlled experiments' (Helm, 1987, p 38).

- It welcomes the checking of provisional findings. We might say 'that although objectivity does not ensure investigative success it minimizes (while not eliminating) the effect of human fallibility and so minimizes the prospect of failure' (Helm, 1987, p 35).
- It makes it 'more possible to be surprised by the facts' (Helm, 1987, p 35).
- It provides the means for settling disagreements.

I would add to this the suggestion that it protects just a little against self-indulgent assumptions that our own position is beyond challenge. In so doing, it provides one basis for treating positions and persons with dignity. We pick up a related aspect of this question in the discussion of 'inner' and 'outer' criteria for assessing the merits of social work research in Chapter Eight.

Is social work research particular to the field?

We should notice a question on which there are varying levels of agreement – is social work research distinct and if so to what degree and in what ways? As with many such broad questions – whether social work is scientific or whether it is a profession – 'it all depends' is an obvious reply, at least as a holding operation. For example, an important, indeed valuable feature of occupational or professional groupings such as social work is a persistent spread of disagreement about matters such as professional values, and its relation to the state or to government. Vague terms such as 'postmodernism' or 'liberalism' are exchanged as badges of honour or accusations of bad faith. We touch on the place of controversies in social work in the final chapter, but the enduring character of such exchanges suggests that a detailed consensus is unlikely over how far social work research is distinctive.

Teasing out this question, it is likely that most of those who raise the question have in mind whether social work research is different in some way from research in other professions, or the social sciences and possibly the humanities. It is unlikely that a comparison with what we call the 'natural' sciences would occur in this context. But the question is worth posing if only because it helps to clarify exactly what is at issue when we consider comparisons and contrasts of this kind. There are in fact three different questions:

- Are the **concepts and theories** of social work of a similar or different order to those of the natural sciences?
- Are the **methods of social work research** of a similar or different order to those of the natural sciences?
- In what ways are **the practices of scientific communities** in social work, the social sciences and the natural sciences comparable?

The answers are not always as straightforward as may be assumed. On concepts and theories, in writing about human needs the prominent American social work leader, Charlotte Towle, argued for seeing the child guidance clinic as more of a laboratory than an agency and as having a place in social evolution. In this she was following a lot of early sociologists of the Chicago School, especially Robert Park (Gross, 2010). We may also ask whether 'deeper' presuppositions from the natural sciences may transfer. For example, do understandings of causation work the same in both spheres? The natural and the human sciences both have 'structural' features that may be shared. The early Chicago ecological models of the city were of this order, as is more recent work on systems and ecology.

Research methods do have more obvious differences from the natural sciences, although even here it is possible to find arguments to the contrary. For example, in an article well regarded among advocates of scientific social work, Platt makes his case for the unity of the sciences and bases this on a logic of analytic induction that he calls 'strong inference' (Platt, 1964, p 347). Here we face the big question of whether all sciences have a unity. There are obvious differences of practice, for example between laboratory-based research and surveys. But differences of methodology and methods follow in part from what Giddens calls the double hermeneutic (Giddens, 1993). In the social sciences, in order to describe 'what someone is doing' in any given context means knowing what the agents themselves know – it depends on 'mutual knowledge' shared by social scientists and the participants. 'The relation between the natural scientist and his or her field of investigation ... is neither constituted nor mediated by mutual knowledge' (Giddens, 1993, p 14).

We should conclude from these paragraphs that social work and social work research will be the poorer if we over-emphasise their distinctiveness. It will make us disinclined to listen to the voices of colleagues in other disciplines and professions. But we can draw on a credible rationale to conceptualise social work research as being committed in a distinctive way to evidence, learning/reflection and emancipation, but without having to set these commitments in a universal or even usual hierarchy that applies in all cases. In summary, social work research should demonstrate a highly rigorous theorising and conceptualisation, and, where empirically based, inquiry strategy and/or methodology. Appropriate research will make an important contribution to social work research knowledge and understanding. It will prove of noted significance for and relevance to social work.

We return to the interrelations between these themes in the final chapter. Because of these different commitments, there will be inevitable tensions. Also even *within* general positions (for example, a commitment to evidence, or to justice-based research) there will be differences. For instance, social work research will be *diverse* but ought to be *coherent*; and it should be *critical* but in a general way *comprehensive*. The strains often surface in relation to the practice role and the researcher. This was captured well by Dannie Abse, the Welsh poet and doctor, in his poem *Song for Pythagoras*:

> White coat and purple coat
> can each be worn in turn;
> but in the white a man will freeze
> and in the purple burn. (Abse, 1989)

One of the main differences we encounter between discipline descriptions in the social sciences is how far the nature of the area is described in terms of understanding/theorising and how far it also includes some notion of 'application'. To take one attempt at specifying social work research,[5] in addition to fairly extensive generic research methods practices, students undertaking research training in social work were expected to demonstrate:

- awareness of and sensitivity to the ethical and governance aspects of their research;
- reflexivity about their own and others' roles in the research process;
- knowledge of the social and political contexts and uses of research;
- knowledge of and sensitivity to conducting research in emancipatory ways.

Much of the content of the first three points could be found in any social science 'benchmark' description of research, but we are being told here that these issues may take special 'shape' in social work. The

---

[5] Taken from a now superseded document setting out the research training requirements for social work doctoral students in the UK.

fourth point is, beyond reasonable contradiction, an area that is stressed more heavily in social work than in any other discipline and in most not at all. But while it makes some degree of sense to ask what is distinctive about social work research, the more significant question is what might make social work research distinctively *good* (Shaw, 2007)?

This does not mean that there is no point in talking about *social work* research. We will see in Chapter Four that the kinds of questions to which social work research is applied do have a distinctive character, although once again care is needed, because the way such questions are prioritised will differ between social work practitioners, service users and social work faculty. In the traditional sciences, there often are debates about whether the key concepts and categories of one science can be expressed through the key categories of another science. Put too simply, this often is expressed as whether the fundamental elements of science are those of physics or perhaps mathematics. Social work should not feel defensive on this. It will help to see how scientists working in the established sciences have countered the reductionist argument. The theoretical chemist Roald Hoffmann said:

> I think reductionism is unrealistic, it's just an ideology that science has bought.... [E]ven within two fields as close to each other as chemistry and physics, embedded at the heart of science, there are concepts in chemistry which are ... not reducible to those in physics, or if they are so reduced they lose ... everything that's interesting about them. (in Wolpert and Richards, 1997, p 22)

Richard Lewontin, an evolutionary biologist, sets the issues out in the following way:

> When scientists break up the world into bits and pieces, they think they're breaking things up into some natural entities, but they're not. They're breaking them up into the bits and pieces they see in the world by their own training; by their own ideology; by the whole way they've been taught to see the world. But that doesn't mean those bits and pieces are the real bits and pieces. So, an anti-reductionist is someone who believes that in order to understand processes of nature, you must not import into them some artificial notion of 'real' bits and pieces. (Cited in Wolpert and Richards, 1997, p 103)

The interviewer here, Wolpert, suggested that he is almost a relativist, taking the view 'that science isn't very special knowledge, but it's just merely another manifestation of the social environment in which we live', to which Lewontin replied: 'But that's because you are a reductionist, and therefore you want to say, either it's objective knowledge, or it's a manifestation of the social milieu' and says he needs to more dialectical (p 108). I find this argument helpful in two ways. First, it makes clear the weakness of reductionist arguments that may come to social work via psychology, neuroscience and the like. Second, it cautions social workers to guard against the same either/or position that Lewontin rightly rejects. Any argument that takes the form of saying that something is 'nothing but' such and such should be treated with great caution at best.[6]

Listening to researchers making judgements

One of the benefits of including several quotations from people working in the mainstream sciences in this and elsewhere in the book is that we gain a greater sense of spontaneous thinking that has not gone through the process of being formalised for the printed page. In Boxes 1.1 and 1.2, we can see social work academics doing something rather similar. An international panel of social work scholars from 14 different countries was asked to identify a number of research studies that, in their own field of social work, they judged to be among the most important ever published. They were invited to give the reasons why they wanted to recommend particular articles.[7] It does not matter which particular articles they were talking about, but it illustrates the criteria they were applying in making their positive appraisals. I introduce them here because I believe they are helpful ways of making a case for the merits of social work research. The emphases have been added.

---

[6] It is interesting that the communications scientist and Christian philosopher of science Donald MacKay adopted the same argument, calling reducing explanations to one key level 'nothing-buttery'. We need 'a whole hierarchy of levels and categories of explanation if we are to do justice to the richness of the nature of man' (MacKay, 1979, p 28).

[7] This was the first stage of assembling a four-volume collection of such articles (Shaw et al, 2016).

Box 1.1: Making a case for the merits of research (1)

1. 'This article is about short narratives about work identity as told by clients. The function of the narratives is to shed light on the consequences of employment-oriented social work as seen from the perspective of the users. The central argument of the article is that the primary producers of the everyday practice of social work, i.e. professionals and clients/users/citizens, have a privileged knowledge, although their knowledge is not the only one of relevance. However, an important place to start, when researching the knowledge base of social work might be to look inside professional practice for the knowledge produced and applied in participants' contributions. *The importance of the article lies in the suggested methodological position, which is to consider practice as matters of translation, mirrored in narratives and accounts by participants, rather than matters of causality.*'

2. 'XXX made several substantial contributions to the general debate on science and social work. This is one of his *mature* considerations not long before his death. If we broadly distinguish stances in relation to science, XXX would occupy a pluralist and pragmatic position that affords authority to science as a development of ordinary thinking; and partly on that premise has a basis for rapprochement with other positions, while retaining a commitment to the power of research. He regards the scientific method as "a specialized tool for determining truth when ordinary means of inquiry do not suffice, but still can be seen as an elaboration of these means" and holds to a progressive view of knowledge as when he says that "in the domain of complex questions for which data can provide answers, scientific methods may well provide the best knowledge simply because they have been developed over time to do just that." In this regard his position is perhaps the most *articulate* statement of this mainstream position.'

Note that in both the examples in Box 1.1, the writers give more space to describing what they regard as the essential elements in the article than to directly evaluative remarks. Even though they are trying to persuade the project editors to include this article, they allow the argument for its merits to emerge from the account of the content and more especially the way the original author/s exemplifies or demonstrates a particular standpoint. That seems a helpful way of deliberating about research, and one that avoids undue partisanship.

Box 1.2: Making a case for the merits of research (2)

3. 'This is *one of the first attempts to get serious about epistemology* and social work. Drawing a wide range of social theories, the paper explores how social work knowledge is socially located and thus socially constructed. For the first time, this paper gave *a sustained and sophisticated voice to social theory and social work*, but without reducing people to objects. "It is a central hypothesis of this paper that social work does have a special regime of truth ... a particular form of knowledge.... Social work ... is concerned to produce knowledge of man as a subject".'

4. 'Appearing in the very first year of publication of the *British Journal of Social Work* this article has significance because it *engages with debates that resonate 40 years on*. First it responds to the requirement that social work demonstrates its effectiveness by producing "results". Second it acknowledges that applying "scientific" evaluation to social work, raises particular issues for social work. Third, and what I consider one of the greatest conundrums for social work, it explores how to research casework i.e. the close interpersonal interventions that constitute social work practice. It does not solve the conundrum – but *initiated the debate*.'

These latter two examples are rather similar to the first pair in the way they avoid very explicit evaluative comments, but express how they see the value of each one by giving a précis of key elements. But they also convey a further reason why these articles merit inclusion – that they are early benchmark contributions that set the tone and agenda, in ways that create an enduring programme. One further characteristic that can be seen in examples 2 and 3 is that, even in a very brief text, direct quotations are given from the original authors. The implication seems to be that these articles speak for themselves – something that can be said of the way all four cases are made.

TWO

Why do research in social work?

We open this chapter by distinguishing different ways we can understand the purpose of social work research, giving examples from the literature. Having recognised a range of appropriate purposes for doing research, we briefly consider the consequence of this for how we deal with the tensions between these purposes. We follow this with a more detailed case example from the work of the reformist evaluation scholar, Ernest House.

From there we will consider how the presence of multiple purposes, sometimes in tension with one another, raises the question of how the purposes of social work research are or should be taken forward by collaborative, cooperative work. While collaboration may seem an obvious virtue, we will see that its achievement is not straightforward. One of the difficulties stems from how best to understand the relationship between social work in the academy and social work in the 'outside world'. We outline how best to understand the role of social work in the academy, and draw the chapter together by suggesting the benefits of borrowing from debates in sociology to develop the idea of a 'public social work'.

We noticed at the beginning of the book that when we come to talk about the *nature* of social work or research we often find ourselves asking what its purpose is. We saw this is the mission statements of the European Social Work Research Association and the Society for Social Work and Research. 'Nature' and 'purpose' are not, of course, the only broad questions we might ask. In talking about this question, I think it is helpful to ask four questions:

- What are the **role** and **purpose** of social work research?
- What **contexts** shape the practice and purpose of social work research?
- How can we maximise the quality of the **practice and method** of social work research?
- How can the aims of social work in its varied **domains** be met through social work research?

The first and to some degree the fourth of these questions provide the focus for this chapter. On the first question, while there is no unanimity on the best balance of purposes, they will typically include one or more of the following:

- generating or enhancing theory and knowledge about social work and social care;
- providing impartial evidence about and for decision making;
- instrumentally improving practice and organisational learning;
- highlighting the quality of lived experience and advancing practice wisdom
- promoting justice, social change and social inclusion.

It might help to give brief examples of each of these, although usually research writers are trying to achieve more than one purpose.

Enhancing theory and knowledge about social work and social care covers a very broad span, and it is almost redundant to list examples. Orme and Briar-Lawson (2010) give a good overview of the question, and it is an area where social work and social policy research overlap. Gal and Weiss-Gal (2017) give an international review of the involvement of social work academics in the policy field. Høgsbro and Shaw (2017) include a number of research examples, from Denmark and elsewhere, about social work within a state context.

Somewhat paradoxically, it is slightly easier to find arguments that research should seek to **find evidence** than it is to locate actual instances of doing so. Two good general discussions are found in the work of Macdonald and Popay (2010) and in chapters one and seven of Kirk and Reid (2002). An important, but more demanding contribution has been made by Mullen (2016). Experimental and quasi-experimental designs, and randomised control trials, are the best-known research approaches geared to evidence finding, though many questions can never be studied through such designs. Research studies that search for rigorous evidence are often brought together through systematic reviews, which sometimes are regarded as themselves a research method.

Organisational learning has become a specialist field, to which some social work researchers have contributed. An overview can be found in the online *Encyclopedia of social work*.[1] One of the more comprehensive social work sources dates from an edited collection

---

[1] http://socialwork.oxfordre.com/view/10.1093/acrefore/9780199975839
.001.0001/acrefore-9780199975839-e-273

published a few years ago (Gould and Baldwin, 2004), and remains a safe guide.

Scott's article (1990) remains one of the most impartial arguments about research on **lived experience and practice wisdom**. Mafile'o (2004) gives an excellent example from her PhD research about Tongan social work. Schön's book, *The reflective practitioner*, has rightly become a classic text (Schön, 1983), and can easily be found through online sites. His ideas also have influenced thinking about learning organisations.

Research on issues of **justice** often deals with various levels of argument for the democratisation of research. A seminar report that covers the range of such positions can be downloaded from the Joseph Rowntree Foundation website.[2] In addition, an old article by the late Bob Holman repays a visit and is well worth reading (Holman, 1987). Pease gives a cogent overview (Pease, 2010) and Lorenz has written helpfully in this area in various places.

There are obvious tensions in thinking about how easy – or perhaps desirable – it is to address more than one purpose. What does all this imply? We live day by day with two ways in which we accept kinds of difference that are part of our approach to social work and research, and which we acknowledge as difficult.

- First, we think of social science research in terms of whether it is applied or not – whether it is undertaken with the intention of being fairly directly helpful in some way. We consider this question in the next chapter.
- Second, and not altogether differently, we often speak in terms of polarities such as truth versus advocacy; policy-relevant research versus critical research; rigour versus relevance; postmodernism versus some forms of rationalism; constructivism versus realism.

On the second point – that regarding our tendency to see the issues in terms of various polarities – the approach taken throughout this book has three strands. First, tensions such as these are real. Second, they cannot and certainly should not be dissolved by the application of some social work chemistry of 'eclecticism', or in research strategy terms through the application of mixed methods of inquiry. Mixed methods have their place, but not if their adoption is premised on the assumption that multiple methods are like parts of a jigsaw that by their very multiplicity allow us to piece together the whole picture.

[2]   www.jrf.org.uk/report/user-involvement-research-building-experience-and-developing-standards Accessed 3 March 2017.

Third, notwithstanding their powerful reality, we should not regard such polarities as based on a fundamental incompatibility derived from different worldviews and philosophies, and hence making impossible any mutuality or meaningful conversation and resolution across the borderlines of difference and disagreement. To adopt the helpful shorthand term, they are not based on philosophical incommensurability.

Task Box 2.1: Incommensurability and paradigms

The currency of the idea of incommensurability became widely distributed in the aftermath of Thomas Kuhn's famous book, *The structure of scientific revolutions*, which first came out in 1962 (Kuhn, 1970). The frequent companion term – and one more commonly encountered in social work – is 'paradigm'. Both are widely misunderstood, and hence their value is undermined. Nothing beats going to the source and actually reading Kuhn.

Many of our decisions and discussions are influenced by where we stand on these issues – in sum, questions of evidence, of understanding and of justice. One reason why we find the range of research purposes given here to be helpful is the way they invite subsequent questions – they open up rather than close down discussion. Rather than run through a sketch of all the issues, the following section focuses on one person – Ernest House, the American evaluation scholar. Along with Lee Cronbach and Donald Campbell who figure elsewhere in this book, House is interesting not only because he has thoughtful and provoking things to say, but also because, like in particular Cronbach, he is largely unknown to social work. He has worked out his position in the field of education and how it is best evaluated. His work thus comes with a mix of freshness and relevance to social work.

Ernest House: reformist evaluation for social justice

It may give a steer to the following paragraphs to think of the key phrases and ideas in House's work as including: persuasion and argumentation; normative considerations; social justice; fair evaluation; impartiality; scientific realism; and causal inference. Each point he makes stimulates us to ask what that implies if carried over to social work.

House is not happy with most approaches to evaluation on three counts. First, their value positions are subjectivist. Whether they are directed at managers, professional elites, or consumers, they distance evaluation from prescriptive recommendations. Second, their epistemology is either objectivist or intuitionist – in other words, they occupy extreme poles on the nature of knowledge. Third, their political assumptions are uniformly pluralist. While he does not level a charge of political complacency, he complains that they are all based on essentially enlightenment philosophies. 'All assume that increased knowledge will make people happy or better satisfied in some way' (House, 1980, p 64).

House's most developed response is captured in his major book, *Evaluating with validity* (House, 1980) and is threefold. First, he argues that the logic of evaluation is not so much rational evidence, but persuasion and argumentation. Evaluations never yield certain knowledge. 'Subjected to serious scrutiny, evaluations always appear equivocal.' The aspiration after certain knowledge 'results from confusing rationality with logic. They are not identical.' 'Evaluations can be no more than acts of persuasion' (p 72). They are acts of argumentation, not demonstration. This is as true for both quantitative and qualitative research methods, despite the fact that 'statistical metaphors' 'give a semblance of certainty and unequivocality to evidence' (p 74). In summary, 'Evaluation persuades rather than convinces, argues rather than demonstrates, is credible rather than certain, is variably accepted rather than compelling' (p 73). House characteristically interleaves considerations of logic and moral positions. He repeatedly claims that normative considerations have been neglected and that 'if this is a weakness in the conduct of science, in evaluation it is a fatal flaw' (House, 1980, p 251).

Second, House has developed extensive arguments for a reformist, social justice purpose for evaluation. He is not indifferent to the aesthetics of evaluation, yet for him, 'Truth is more important than beauty. And justice more important than either' (p 117). Utilitarian theories of justice, based on the greatest net satisfaction, provide clear criteria for evaluating, yet tend to favour the upper classes, lead to judgements that 'do not square with one's moral sensibilities' (p 134), and often are marked by oversimplification. Pluralist and intuitionist theory comes closest to common-sense, everyday judgements of justice, and fosters a valuable emphasis on portraying the opinions of stakeholders. Yet 'the threat of relativism' (p 134) jeopardises consistency of application, and it tends to place too high a value on professional judgement.

> In essence, the pluralist model confuses issues of interests with conflicts of power. It can balance only those interests that are represented – typically those of the powerful. (House, 1991a, p 240)

House's conception of justice finds its most practical application in his detailed arguments for a fair evaluation agreement (1980, chapter eight; these are set out in Chapter Eight of this book), and in his broader arguments for evaluation ethics (see, for example, House, 1993). His replacement of traditional ideas of objectivity with impartiality undergirds his explicit reformist stance. In responding to mainstream criticisms that his fair evaluation agreement is biased towards the interests of the disadvantaged, he replies:

> It seems to me that making certain the interests of the disadvantaged are represented and seriously considered is not being biased, though it is certainly more egalitarian than much current practice. (1991a, pp 241-2)

Third, House seeks to resolve the epistemological problems of preceding evaluation approaches through a sophisticated scientific realism, which he hopes may offer the basis of a new synthesis for resolving 'paradigm wars' within evaluation (House, 1991b). His scientific realism involves understandings of 'cause' and 'objectivity' that are very different to conventional ideas. In this respect, he anticipates later developments of scientific realism that sometimes have been applied to social work (for example, Blom and Morén, 2010). He has also sought to integrate evaluative logic and justice, in order to develop a basis for synthesising evaluation results (House, 1995).

His approach to justice issues has loopholes, which he generally acknowledges. His major work was completed when neo-Marxist applications of justice were still emerging, and before sustained feminist work had been undertaken. He is well aware that the underlying assumptions of such positions are different from both his own and those of his theoretical predecessors. He does tend to assume an overly consensual view of society, which limits his reformist position. He believes that, although philosophers, legislators and the public disagree, they do so 'within the frameworks of overall agreement about fundamental democratic values' (1995, p 44). His commitment to participatory models of evaluation is shaped by his retention of an expert evaluator role.

The agenda he drafts for how we carry out research is extensive. His thinking on justice is subtle, whether he warns that research practice is not *determined* by our views of justice, or when he distinguishes between cultural and moral relativity in accepting the proper diversity of concepts of justice. Taken together, the work of House, Cronbach and Campbell provides a well-anchored platform for causal inferences. Programmes are not fixed entities that 'play statue' (in Cronbach's phrase), but vary from site to site. Causes are discovered by knowledge of particulars – 'evaluation approaches that expect and track variability and irregularity of events' (House, 1991b, p 8). Qualitative methodology offers his approach of choice in such circumstances, although not exclusively. He has worked consistently with his own aspiration for 'a more complete and more translucent conceptual order and ... a stronger sense of moral responsibility' (1980, p 11).

Task Box 2.2: House and social work

A good basis for extending this partly developed case study of House's ideas would be to read one of the cited House sources and consider ways in which positive applications to social work may be drawn out.

Collaboration and cooperation

The presence of multiple purposes, sometimes in tension with one another, raises the question of how the purposes of social work research are or should be taken forward by collaborative, cooperative work. It also raises questions of disagreements and controversies. We deal with the second issue towards the close of the book. The desirability of collaborative endeavour may seem to be a given, yet 'tensions and paradoxes are essential features of collaboration, even within established, co-located research groups, so the mere occurrence of face-to-face interaction does not insure that understanding and solidarity will result' (Hackett, 2005, p 668). Hackett expresses these tensions as 'openness and secrecy, cooperation and competition, priority and patience, dirigisme and autonomy, craft and articulation work, role conflicts, and risks of various sorts' (p 670).

Hackett suggests that the questions concerning what collaboration is, and why scientists should collaborate, are 'deceptively simple questions' that 'have elicited complicated and qualified answers' (p 668). He makes a series of distinctions that are valuable in untangling these and other questions. These include:

> *extent*, measured as a distribution over substantive, social, or geographic space, or over time; *intensity*, measured as the frequency or significance of interaction among persons, places, or units of time; *substance*, or the aims and content of collaborative work, which now include producing fundamental knowledge, developing technologies, guiding decisions, making things, training, and bonding; *heterogeneity*, or the variety of participants, purposes, languages (ethnic, national, disciplinary, sectoral), and modalities of collaboration (face-to-face, electronically mediated in various ways, and episodic); *velocity*, or the rate at which results are produced, analyzed, interpreted, and published; *formality*, ranging from contractual arrangements among nations or organizations to handshake agreements and unstated understandings among friends and acquaintances. (Hackett, 2005, p 669; emphasis added)

National boundaries, even where first languages are shared, are also likely to shape the extent to which forms of collaboration occur. This offers an agenda for social work and 'theories of innovation and social networks could benefit from further investigations of how weak ties change into strong ties during the collaboration process' (Cummings and Kiesler, 2005, pp 717-18). 'Currently we have no theory of the "ideal" level of collaboration in science' and 'in future research we should examine how different kinds of science use different forms of collaboration' (p 718).

As we consider this, it is important to recognise that professional work of any kind is marked by social interests. How do social interests shape social work research? Within this are two questions. First, how convincingly may we, by doing science, claim to understand something or someone's interests as well as or better than do they? Second, what should we make of the argument that the processes, results, outcomes and applications of science are shaped as much, or even more, by collective interests than by rationality?

On the first, what if we suspect participants misunderstand their form of life? Kemp says, 'the question is whether social scientists can ever justifiably claim to understand actors' interests better than those actors do themselves' (2012, p 664). Kemp is speaking of social scientists, but we may ask the same of social workers. My hunch is that most social workers will respond to this question with a categorical 'No.' Defences of the position that actors' perceptions of their interests cannot be challenged have been made on grounds such as the habitual, intractable nature of subjective preferences, the non-objective character of normative judgements, or the centrality of actors' understandings in constituting the world (Woolgar, 1981). Those who believe an objective evaluation of actors' judgements can be made have been criticised, for example, for imposing their values on others. On the other hand, those who think actors' judgements are beyond challenge or change have been accused of conservatism.[3] This non-judgemental position says that where there is a clash between social work researchers' and research participants' views of their interests, we should always accept the latter. It is possible to find statements of this position among those who are committed to emancipatory and user-led research.

On the contrary, Kemp suggests that it is possible, in certain circumstances, for social scientists to justify the preferable character of their accounts of interests. Social scientists 'should attempt to demonstrate the value of social scientific understandings by identifying difficulties and problems that lay actors have been experiencing as a result of acting on their own problematic understandings, and showing how social scientific understandings can resolve these' (2012, p 673).

What of the second question, whether social work and research is influenced more by collective interest than rationality? At one level, this is a relatively modest position, to the effect that the production of new ideas is socially influenced, but these ideas are then judged by scientific criteria – a position not unlike that taken by Weber. However, it is possible to radicalise the argument and reason that not only the production of new ideas, but also the process by which those ideas are accepted or rejected can be affected by social factors. The issue is whether or not it helps to distinguish the politics of science and the truth of science, and should knowledge claims regarded as true be explained differently from knowledge claims regarded as false? Witkin seems to say no to both questions when he suggests that 'There is no intrinsic reason, apart from the interests of particular groups ... to limit knowledge claims to certain criteria' (Witkin, 1999, p 7).

To lay my cards on the table, I accept the distinction between politics claims and truth claims in social work research, but concur with Phillips when he says that it 'is a rough or permeable distinction rather than a watertight one' (Phillips, 2000, p 206).

---

[3]   Paradoxically, this has sometimes been supported in social work on the grounds that it is a radical position.

Social work in the academy

The book by Gal and Weiss-Gal, recommended earlier, is titled *Where academia and policy meet* (Gal and Weiss-Gal, 2017). While the 'academia' part may seem unduly restrictive, there lies beneath such a collection the question of whether conventional ways of seeing the research–practice relationship are appropriate for professions within universities and colleges. There are two ways in which practice becomes problematic in the academy. First, there is a misleading set of assumptions about the application of knowledge, which complicates efforts to make sense of what counts as doing social work within the academy, whether by academic faculty or students. Second, the characteristic university career mode for social work poses distinctive difficulties related to moving from professional practice outside the university to such practice inside the university.

On the first point, the problem stems to a significant degree from the low esteem afforded to manual labour and, in turn, to applied science as far back as Plato, who sought to separate experimental and applied science from pure science. 'Only in medicine was manual work really honoured by the Greeks' (Hooykaas, 1972, p 80). There are echoes of this in some contemporary conceptions of evidence-based practice. Hooykaas approvingly quoted Thomas Spratt, the 18th-century author of *The history of the Royal Society of London*, saying 'philosophy will then attain to perfection, when either the Mechanic labourers shall have philosophical heads, or the Philosophers shall have mechanical hands' (Hooykaas, 172, p 96).

I think we could seek to understand social work research in universities in terms of the occupational socialisation of social work faculty members in the academy. One way of doing this was taken up some time ago by Becker and Carper in developing the idea of 'commitment' as part of an occupational identity and career. It seems a plausible assumption that occupational identity for social work academics and researchers will not be the same as that for practitioners. This simple notion points to an understanding of one reason why research–practice relations in social work are difficult – that is, that separate occupational cultures exist and indeed become established as entailing a set of contrasting commitments.

How practice and research are seen in social work should not be viewed in a static way. Changes in identity occur *via* various mechanisms. These include 'the development of problem interest and pride in new skills, the acquisition of professional ideology, investment, the internalization of motives, and sponsorship' (Becker and Carper,

1970 [1956], p 198). We also need to take into account that such change may produce *conflict* where an individual ends up with either one element of occupational identity incongruent with others or indeed the occupational identity in conflict with, for example, family and wider social identity (Becker and Carper, 1970 [1957]).

We can reasonably hypothesise that making a commitment to engaging with research has costs for a social worker in the academy – it may violate expectations of the wider occupational community, and lead to occupation change with risks of abandoning earlier career 'investments'. It may entail costs such as loss of social network connections or of status. The adjustment in career interests also may entail loss through 'unfitting' oneself for other future positions. Becker takes from Goffman's analysis of face-to-face interaction the idea that a front – a 'safe face' – developed to support one identity may be lost by a shift to new identity. For example, in social work, a commitment to advocacy on behalf of service users may be lost in research situations where stances of impartiality may be valued and expected. A further element is that what is valued varies in sub-cultures *within*, for example, a practice or academic community (Shaw and Norton, 2008). Finally, in social work, the move to university typically occurs after a lengthy period in practice, where such commitments have become established, and hence pressure to continue to act consistently with those will be considerable (compare Becker, [1970 (1960)], p 285).

My suspicion is that neither academic colleagues nor social work employers are ready enough to recognise the reality and significance of questions of identity, and how they are shaped in enduring ways by someone's occupational domicile.

Is there a case for a public social work?

There has been an ongoing debate in sociology about relationships between professions, the academy and the world, which has relevance and partial transferability to how we understand the purposes of social work research. Michael Burawoy's 2004 presidential address to the American Sociological Association on 'public sociology' set it going (Burawoy, 2005). While it is a rather insular argument, perhaps inconsistently focused only on sociology insiders, it calls for attention by social workers. Burawoy argues that 'In its beginning sociology aspired to be … an angel of history, searching for order in the broken fragments of modernity, seeking to salvage the promise of progress' (Burawoy, 2005, p 5). However, 'If our predecessors set out to change the world we have too often ended up conserving it. Fighting for a place in the academic sun, sociology developed its own specialized knowledge...' (Burawoy, 2005, p 5; compare Fuller, 2006).

Central to Burawoy's argument is his lament relating to an 'antagonistic interdependence among four types of knowledge: professional, critical, policy, and public' (2005, p 4). 'Public sociology brings sociology into a conversation with publics, understood as people who are themselves involved in conversation' (p 7). Burawoy wants to place the questions 'for whom and for what do we pursue sociology?' at the centre of the discipline. 'Herein lies the promise and challenge of public sociology, the complement and not the negation of professional sociology' (p 5).

Social work voices sometimes have been heard sending up a corresponding lament (see, for example, Specht and Courtney, 1994). In a social work context, a public social work would promote an organic social work in which social work scholars – or at least a significant part of that community – work in close connection with a 'visible, thick, active, local and often counterpublic' (Burawoy, 2005, p 7). This might include neighbourhood associations, communities of faith, immigrant rights groups and human rights organisations. 'Between the organic public sociologist and a public is a dialogue, a process of mutual education' (Burawoy, 2005, p 8).

In developing this position, we need to distinguish different kinds of knowledge. Thomas Schwandt (1997) distinguishes between theoretical knowledge ('knowing that'), craft or skill knowledge ('knowing how') and practical–moral knowledge ('knowing from'). It is this third form of knowledge that is central to developing a public social work. For Schwandt, when we talk about 'application', something more is intended than the instrumental sense of practicality (as though a social work model of intervention or a finding about effectiveness could be applied like a 'tool') – that is, the more fundamental sense of making something relevant to oneself. This involves a particular kind of knowledge – 'knowing from within or practical–moral knowledge', which 'requires not cleverness in application but understanding' (Schwandt, 1997, p 76). 'Practical–moral knowledge aims to actually move people, not simply give them good ideas' (p 81).

We should not slip into romanticism. Each kind of social work knowledge and practice can assume pathological forms. By way of analogy once more with public sociology, each type of social work has its own legitimation: disciplinary social work justifies itself on the basis of scientific norms, policy-oriented social work on the basis of its effectiveness, critical social work on the basis of its ability to supply moral visions, and public social work on the basis of its relevance. Each has its own forms of accountability and politics, and each its own form of pathology, whether it be insularity and irrelevance for disciplinary social work, sectarianism in the case of critical social work, contractual distortions within policy-oriented social work, or hostages to the pursuit of acceptability and popularity, or risk of speaking down to its publics, within public social work. The varied and sometimes contradictory elements inherent in the two primary senses of academisation – both being taught in the academy and carrying expectations of a research culture – means that social work practitioners, agencies and 'academics' should not assume that a balanced 'treaty' is easily mapped out or achieved.

This brings us to wider questions about the application of social work research, and we turn to these in the next chapter. As we do so, we draw out more explicitly a remark in Chapter One about three standards relating to how we should endeavour to accomplish the evidential, understanding and justice purpose of research:

- Social work research should demonstrate a highly rigorous theorising and conceptualisation, and, where empirically based, inquiry strategy and/or methodology.
- It should endeavour to make an important contribution to social work research knowledge and understanding.
- If successful in so doing, it will prove of noted significance for and relevance to social work. Explicitly or implicitly it will yield gains for a justice-based social work.

I would add one final caveat. Generally speaking, these purposes and the means of their accomplishment are not ones that can or even ought to be applied to each and every individual research initiative. The responsibility of the social work community in this regard is a collective one.

THREE

Doing research application

We begin this chapter by developing several ways in which social work can be understood as being concerned with applying what we know. I will aim to show that the question of 'application' is more difficult than we often realise. We then will work through recent discussions of the meaning and importance of the 'impact' of research. Moving on from there we will take as a social work example the question of doing 'practitioner research'. We will learn more about the nature of practitioner research in the next chapter. In this chapter, the emphasis will be on what we know about the *experience* of doing practitioner research. The opening part of the chapter is the most difficult so it may help to jump to the section on the impact of research and come back to this opening part after finishing the rest of the chapter.

> In a very broad sense, social work research is the application of research methods to solve problems that social workers confront in the practice of social work. It provides information that can be taken into consideration by social workers prior to making decisions that affect their clients, programmes or agencies such as use of alternative intervention techniques or change or modification of programme/client/objectives and so forth.[1]

A definition of social work research in terms such as these will be taken almost as a given. It is about the application of methods and information for the solving of problems in the lives of those with whom social work practitioners work from day to day. To hesitate or seem to cast doubt appears almost a betrayal. In one such act of apparent disloyalty, Noel Timms confessed his 'delineation of social work as concerned with understanding rather than information, and understanding not necessarily with a "practical" or predetermined end in view' (Timms, 1972, pp 1-2). 'We should consider social work as primarily neither

[1] Samuel, R. 2011 'Meaning of social work research.' Available at www.scribd.com/doc/46696769/Meaning-of-Social-Work-Research

an applied science nor simple good works but a kind of practical philosophising' (p 3). Recognising the serious intent that lies behind Timms' remarks, we explore how 'practice', and the process of applying what we know, is more difficult than we may expect.

Practice

The American sociologist C. Wright Mills bequeathed a notable – well, notorious – critique of social pathologists, among whom he numbered social workers (Mills, 1943). Textbooks are in his firing line. He talks through how the selection of what to include is not random, but exhibits a professional ideology: 'The direction is definitely toward particular "practical problems" – problems of "everyday life."' He is critical of how 'The ideal of practicality, of not being "utopian," operated, in conjunction with other factors, as a polemic against the "philosophy of history"' (Mills, 1943, p 168). The 'survey' style of textbooks undergirds 'an epistemology of gross description', which then lingers in an academic tradition. 'The emphasis on fragmentary practical problems tends to atomize social objectives' (p 168-9), such that 'There are few attempts to explain deviations from norms in terms of the norms themselves' (p 169). As he puts it, 'The focus on "the facts" takes no cognizance of the normative structures within which they lie' (p 169). He chooses to illustrate this from social work and Mary Richmond's 1917 book, *Social diagnosis* – possibly the most famous single social work book of all time – of which he remarks:

> Present institutions train several types of persons – such as judges and social workers – to think in terms of 'situations'. Their activities and mental outlook are set within the existent norms of society; in their professional work they tend to have an occupationally trained incapacity to rise above series of 'cases'. It is in part through such concepts as 'situation' and through such methods as 'the case approach' that social pathologists have been intellectually tied to social work with its occupational position and political limitations. (p 171)

Theory

Can we offer a defensible response to this kind of argument – one that continues to rumble along in the social sciences? I think we can. First, some clarification is needed regarding how we think about theory and its relation to practice. The gap between theory and practice is typically formulated as a knowledge-transfer problem, in which practitioners fail to adopt research findings. Social workers often face the 'scholastic fallacies' (Nowotny, 2003, p 156) sometimes evident in the dominance of social science and research 'experts' over practice 'beneficiaries'. As Schön has expressed it:

> Research and practice are presumed to be linked by an exchange in which researchers offer theories and techniques applicable to practice problems, and practitioners, in return, give researchers new problems to work on and practical tests of the utility of research results. (Schön, 1992, p 53)

The word 'theory' is always used in relation to practice as an interaction between things done, things observed and systematic explanation of these. Yet while this requires a distinction, it does not require opposition. We observe this when Popper insists that 'Practice is not the enemy of theoretical knowledge but the most valuable incentive to it' (Popper, 1966, p 222). We can see this helpful position in various ways. For example, the word *praxis* has entered language to suggest a new relation of theory and practice. The sense we give it is of 'practice informed by theory' intended to unite theory in the sense of explanation and a scheme of ideas with a strong sense of 'practical', that is, practice in action.

A further helpful position is present from ways in which the understanding of the relationship of theory and practice has been shaped by a resurgence of interest in Aristotelian approaches to ethics, marked by deliberative reasoning and case-by-case decisions through a process of practical wisdom or *phronesis*. Schwandt concludes:

> When confronted with a knowledge claim the pragmatist is less concerned with whether it is right and asks instead, 'What would I be committing myself to?'... This shifts the focus of inquiry from verification and the appeal to method, to practice and an appeal to deliberation and conversation. (Schwandt, 1993, p 18)

Schwandt elsewhere infers from this position:

> (1) that the social world ... can only be studied from a position of involvement "within" it, instead of as an 'outsider'; (2) that knowledge of that world is practical-

moral knowledge and does not depend upon justification or proof for its practical efficacy; (3) that we are not in an 'ownership' relation to such knowledge but we embody it as part of who and what we are. (Schwandt, 1997, p 75)

We have noted how social workers often face the dominance of social science and research 'experts' over practice 'beneficiaries'. This tends to lead to a deeply unhelpful situation in which practitioners are routinely blamed for their perceived failure to act on the 'findings' of research. A particularly helpful way to counter this tendency was provided by the systems theorist, Norma Romm. Her basic premise is that 'the process of attempting to "know" about the social world already is an intervention in that world which may come to shape its constitution' (Romm, 1995, p 137). Romm says that 'The view that theory is applied in practice and may be tested in that practice, can amount to an unreflected/unreflexive endorsement of a theoretical position' (Romm, 1996, p 25). Further, 'One is not just applying "findings", but intervening in the social discussion in a specific way, that is, in a way which authorises particular conceptions' (p 145).

Research and practice

The practice and theory question of relationship is related, of course, to the parallel question of research and practice. Once again, we should beware too immediate a response that sets the one as distant from the other. Trevillion helpfully asks us to consider whether social work research can be seen as an emergent property of practice. He says:

> To suggest that practice can have a significant formative influence on research is to suggest that we think about research as a particular kind of practice outcome. This is a startling proposition. It runs counter to the rather romantic idea that research is the outcome of an independent community of scholars exploring issues in a process driven exclusively by intellectual curiosity. It also challenges the assumption that the world of research is essentially rational and linear and that the researcher is in control of the research agenda by suggesting that research is a product of the same messy world that social workers and service users inhabit. (Trevillion, 2010, p 168)

Trevillion is not claiming that practice determines the nature of research, but that it is 'rather a way of pointing out that the process of searching for knowledge is itself rooted in the conditions being examined' (2010, p 168). This has some similarity to remarks by Polanyi, who, known in social work mainly for his work on some forms of tacit knowledge, does not strongly separate practical from theoretical knowledge – knowing what and knowing how, *wissen* and *können*. 'These two aspects of knowing have a similar structure and neither is ever present without the other' (Polanyi, 1966, p 20).

I find this kind of head-over-heels argument refreshing and pointed, in that it challenges the usual top-down assumption that research is autonomous and drives social work practice, while being untouched by that same practice. Extending how we should think about practice, Sheila Spong seeks to resolve the theory–practice dualism in her helpful reflections on counselling (Spong, 2007). She argues that effective relationship-based practice requires what she calls pragmatic belief, which obliges the practitioner 'to hold in tension the belief needed for therapy to be effective and the scepticism required to maintain openness to alternative interpretations' (2007, p 55). This entails an ability to retain 'an "as-if" position: ... immersed but not absorbed; ... utterly present and to have a meta-view, understanding that there are other possibilities and perspectives' (p 62).

Drawing this section together, research and practice need linking in ways that release the potential for practice to challenge social work science, and in so doing to contest conventional hierarchical ways of seeing expert–beneficiary relationships. When theory–practice relationships are viewed as the failure of practitioners to apply the theories developed by those who are engaged in empirical and theoretical pursuits, this distorts reality. To regard theory and practice problems as breakdowns in communication that afflict practitioners is to fail to recognise that practical problems of this kind occur in the course of any theoretical undertaking. To assume that they can somehow be identified and tackled in theory and then 'applied' in practice tends to conceal how they are generated out of practice.

We have reached an important realisation about what it means to be 'practical', nowhere better expressed than by Schwab a half century ago when he argued for a language of the practical rather than the theoretical. By practical 'I do *not* mean ... the easily achieved, familiar goals which can be reached by familiar means' (Schwab, 1969, p 1), but rather 'a complex discipline ... concerned with choice and action' (pp 1-2).

Task Box 3.1: Being practical

Take Schwab's comment that by practical we should not mean 'the easily achieved, familiar goals which can be reached by familiar means', but rather 'a complex discipline ... concerned with choice and action'. Think of an instance when you were able, either in social work practice or research, to accomplish something and act in a 'practical' manner. Of what did that 'practical' activity consist?

From this first part of the chapter, we can infer that the assumption that good social work science will always be of direct or indirect value is too simple. The sociologist Robert Merton recognised an intellectual division of labour in science generally, rather than an all-or-nothing commitment to either pure or applied work. Some are suited to the exclusive pursuit of one or the other, 'some may move back and forth between both; and a few may manage to tread a path bordered on one side by the theoretical and on the other by the practical or applied' (Merton, 1971, p 793). Yet it is worth remembering the words of Thomas Spratt, quoted earlier, saying 'philosophy will then attain to perfection, when either the Mechanic labourers shall have philosophical heads, or the Philosophers shall have mechanical hands' (Hooykaas, 1972, p 96).

The 'impact' of research

I am not fond of the word 'impact' in this connection. It implies force, collision, even a blow. But until governments, at least in the English-speaking world, find a more congenial term, we are stuck with it. The general question is by no means limited to social work or even the social sciences. James Lighthill, a prominent applied mathematician, reflected:

> I don't think I've ever solved the classical problem of the interface between science and politics, though I've given a lot of attention to it. I think it's a peculiarly hard interface.... I always felt that there was such an enormous barrier between the way in which politicians look at the world, and the way in which scientists do, that it's very hard to penetrate it. And yet it must be penetrated. (in Wolpert and Richards, 1997, p 66)

When thinking about the uses of research, Kirk and Reid (2002) suggest a six-fold distinction:

- instrumental;
- enlightenment;
- conceptual;
- persuasive;
- methodological;
- indirect, in terms of use that is mediated through, for example, research-based models.

The relationship between research and action cannot be seen simply as 'scientists understand' and then 'social workers do'. Reid described this view of utilisation whereby findings are applied to the solution of a problem as 'instrumental utilisation', and argued that it does not occur very often (Reid, 1988). Probably a more common form of utilisation is 'conceptual utilisation', in which findings are added to a storehouse of information, and emerge at some future point. Then there is what Reid terms 'persuasive utilisation', in which evidence, ideas and understandings are used to advance a point of view. This portrayal of utilisation processes suggests that implementation of research is always likely to be 'murky and convoluted' (Reid, 1988, p 55).

Incidentally, taking this wider understanding of how research may be useful and have worth, we should consider the widespread assumption that quantitative research is always more likely to be of use than qualitative research. In an incisive overview, Jerrim and de Vries set out how, while quantitative social science has the potential to make an important contribution to public policy, it has a number of limitations (Jerrim and de Vries, 2017). Policy makers sometimes seem more readily drawn to quantitative evidence. This may be because 'numerical findings and statistics may seem more certain and "scientific" than qualitative observations and interviews' (Jerrim and de Vries, 2017, p 117). Not only certain, but headline quantitative results seem to enable a grip on complex social problems. Jerrim and de Vries open out several underlying limitations that jeopardise these assumptions, as follows.

- Quantitative research reports often lack the information that allows transparency and verifiability. This is a particular problem, given that mistakes are easy to make and many judgement calls are essential.
- Quantitative evidence is often read as if it is clear and unambiguous. Unfortunately, such findings 'are usually subject to much more

uncertainty than seems to be commonly understood by policy makers' (Jerrim and de Vries, 2017, p 120). Placing disproportionate weight on tests of statistical significance entails neglect of other sources of uncertainty such as measurement error.

- A more general problem is publication bias, when certain kinds of results are more likely to get accepted for publication (or, indeed, submitted for review) than others. Take cognitive behavioural research – in the UK at least, this has had positive support from within governments. It seems clear that journals are more likely to accept research that reports 'positive' findings than research that reports 'negative' results. Researchers are more likely to submit research that reports positive results. It is clear how this may lead to over-reporting of positive results when there may be a hidden body of negative results from unpublished/unsubmitted research.
- Finally, research is accepted following a process of peer review, and there is evidence that levels of agreement between reviewers is not high.

Hammersley (2000) offered a complementary argument by identifying ways in which qualitative research may have value. His immediate focus was on education, but his argument easily transfers to social work.

Qualitative research may be *appreciative*, referring to 'The ability to understand and represent points of view which are often obscured or neglected' (Hammersley, 2000, p 394-5), which 'requires that people's behaviour be understood as making sense in the context in which it occurs' (p 395), and of recognising the rationalities that exist in how service users and social workers act. A problem with mainstream approaches to research use is that they are too closely aligned to a 'correctional' perspective, where the perspectives of the policy enforcement community come to dominate. Qualitative researchers are sometimes accused of taking sides. But 'while partisanship is undoubtedly a danger in appreciative research, it is not automatically built into it' (p 395). 'By contrast, partisanship is built into correctionalism, though this often remains invisible to correctionalists, since they identify their own viewpoint with the public good' (p 396).

Qualitative research also may have use value that is *designatory* – to 'enable people to think consciously what they have been only half aware of' and thus 'finding the most illuminating language with which to describe people's experiences and actions'. Hence, 'by providing a language which conceptualises the tacit knowledge on which teachers rely, qualitative researchers can aid the development of professional knowledge and skills' (p 396). Within a social work context, it can be a way of rendering explicit forms of good practice, in ways exemplified by Neander and Skott (2006), who brought together service users and key 'important persons' whom they had found helpful, to jointly explore what had been effective.

Hammersley also identifies use values that are reflective (holding up a mirror to the educational experience to see what is going on, rather than what is thought to be going on or wished); immunological ('the potential for research to immunise us against grandiose schemes of innovation, against raising expectations or setting targets too high; indeed against the "idolatry of the new" more generally' [Hammersley, 2000, p 398]); and corrective.

We have already heard the gist of Norma Romm's argument that 'practice cannot become the tool to substantiate theory, because *criteria for judging the relevance of practice are already written into the* theory' (Romm, 1996, p 27; emphasis in original). Romm proposes the formula 'comprehension=application'. This says more than application is *based on* comprehension; rather, comprehension is 'inextricably tied to' application (1996, p 26). Romm believes that this formulation 'provides a way of challenging the (excessive) partiality which ensues, ironically, in the quest to ground knowledge in an impartial "inquiry" moment' (p 28). She helpfully insists on 'not suppressing alternative ways of conceiving and seeing the world' and 'the need to be critical or suspicious of our intellectual assumptions' (p 26). So our social work practice decisions 'can be defended only on the grounds that one has *thought-and-acted having taken one's encounter with other arguments and possibilities seriously*' (p 27; emphasis in original). Hence we need a form of discursive accountability in which we 'defend our choices of vision and of action in the light of serious confrontation with alternatives' (p 34).

Lee Cronbach

Reflection on what is entailed in research utilisation is sufficient for us to realise that research to practice perhaps never occurs through formulated rules uniformly implemented across research projects. It is personal confession time. At this point, I want to slow down and introduce someone who is for me a star – Lee Cronbach (1916-2001). Though there is much that could be said about the cogent power of his writing, and to lament that he should be almost totally unknown within social work, I want to take the work of him and a group of his colleagues about evaluation as an exemplar case study of how to think about the influence, power and impressions made by inquiry.[2] While I allow Cronbach to speak largely in his own words, his major book was the result of several years' seminar discussion between evaluators from a variety of disciplines. An important qualification is in order. I regard Cronbach as an exemplar not because I always agree with him, but because he sets out an important case cogently and fully. I have called him elsewhere a 'multi–partisan evaluator' (Shaw, 1999) over more explicitly reformist positions, such as that held by House (Chapter Two, of this book), and very clearly distinct from approaches to evaluation that draw on critical theory.

For Cronbach, the act of inquiry and its impact were inseparable, because 'a theory of evaluation must be as much a theory of political interaction as it is a theory of how knowledge is constructed' (Cronbach et al, 1980, pp 52-3). With characteristic dry wit, he remarks: 'The very proposal to evaluate has political impact. To ask about the virtue of Caesar's wife is to suggest she is not above suspicion' (p 163).

When it came to policy and political change, he was a committed gradualist. His position was to see evaluation as 'handmaiden to gradualism' (p 158). 'Evaluation is both conservative and committed to change.... This is the stance of a friendly critic, not of a person who sees the system as either beyond reproach or beyond repair'. 'To be meliorist is the evaluator's calling. Rarely or never will evaluative work bring a 180-degree turn in social thought. Evaluation assists in piecemeal adaptations: perhaps it does tend to keep the *status* very nearly *quo*' (p 157; emphasis in original).

Even where we may depart from his prescriptions, there is much to gain by understanding his position. '(E)valuators should be contributing to the slow, continuous cumulative understanding of a problem or intervention' (p 47). This stemmed from his beliefs about the role of the evaluator, that within the political climate evaluation's 'role is not to produce authoritative truths but to clarify, to document, to raise new questions, to create new perceptions' (p 53). It is the evaluator's task to illuminate, not to dictate, the decision' (p 155). He insists that 'progress requires that we respect poorly formed and even "untestable" ideas' (Cronbach, 1986, p 86). In a nice phrase, he says: 'We should be stern only where it would cost us much to be wrong' (p 86). He exercises epistemological modesty when he says:

---

[2]   Cronbach also made major contributions to the fields of measurement theory and pedagogy. A brief account of his career can be seen at http://web.stanford.edu/dept/news/pr/01/cornbachobit1010.html.

In my opinion, social science is cumulative, not in possessing ever-more-refined answers about fixed questions, but in possessing an ever-richer repertoire of questions. (p 91)

We do not store up truths or laws. What social scientists mostly harvest are additional concepts and inquiry skills, along with careful records of events observed. (p 104)

Moreover, he says, 'We shall not advise the evaluator to avoid opportunities to be helpful; he is hired to improve public services, not to referee a basketball game' (Cronbach et al, 1980, p 18). The evaluator:

can be an arm of those in power, but he [sic] loses most of his value in that role if he does not think independently and critically. He can put himself in the service of some partisan interest outside the centre of power, but there again his unique contribution is a critical, scholarly habit of mind. (p 67)

This position set him in a very different position from the 'establishment' position of those fashioned by the work of Donald Campbell. 'Evaluation is not best used, we think, to bring pressure on public servants' (p 17). 'We are uneasy about the close association of evaluation with accountability. In many of its uses, the word becomes an incantation and one that can cast a malign spell' (p 133). In terms that anticipate later work on appreciative evaluation, he observes '[a]ccountability is most demanded of those public servants condemned to farm rocky ground, under capricious weather conditions' (p 137).

We reach a core point for Cronbach, and one where his distance from and critique of standard positions on randomised control trials are most clear. '"External validity" – validity of inferences that go beyond the data – is the crux of social action, not "internal validity"'. Internal validity gains may be feasible 'to some extent, but relevance is likely to suffer' (p 231). Cronbach always favours relevance over precision, but does not see them as choices.

This influences how he thinks about the question of utilising research and evaluation. He retains a clear distinction between facts and values, but, unlike other positions, gives weight to each. He and his colleagues offer a framework for thinking about how evaluation use works by taking into account the relationship between the level of community agreement on values and the level of agreement about the facts of the matter.

Figure 3.1: Evaluation use – facts and values

With regard to values

		Consensus	Disagreement
	Consensus	Rational analysis	Compromise
With regard to facts	Disagreement	Judgement	Inspiration

The command/rational model tends to an instrumental view of *use*. Regarding the political process as one of accommodation tends to enlightenment views of use. The gains will be manifest for, if the investigator can keep the image of a reflective and disinterested observer, those with whom he interacts are under some pressure to speak reasonably themselves. Drawing together the implications of viewing the evaluator as public scientist they suggest a set of personal values:

- The evaluator should 'not attempt to evaluate a program with whose basic aims he is not in sympathy' (p 208). *Over*-sympathy is much less a problem as long as one is committed to an effective programme.
- Openness to good and bad news in data collection, and impartiality in interpretation, are important. This is *not* the same as value-neutrality but may be achieved by 'considering the facts from the relevant, no doubt conflicting, perspectives' (p 209).
- In terms akin to Max Weber, Cronbach and colleagues conclude of the evaluator that '[h]aving done his professional job, he puts off his professional robes and, if he chooses, speaks up for what he as a citizen favours' (p 209).

Task Box 3.2: Cronbach for social work

I have left Cronbach to speak almost wholly in his own words, in so doing enabling the use of this exemplar as a basis for group discussion.

How might Cronbach's vision lead to distinctive approaches to the utilisation of social work research and evaluation?

Journals

It is impossible to talk about research impact without noticing the popularity of impact scores and rankings for journals. In case this slightly esoteric process is unfamiliar, this is how it typically is done. The number of times authors of articles published in a given year cited articles in our journal of interest in the two previous years is counted. Then the total number of articles published in the journal for those same years also is counted. The first number is divided by the second number.

A hypothetical example may help. Assume that we are calculating a score for a particular journal for 2017 – let us call it the *International Journal of Welfare Practice*. We find that articles published in our journal of interest were cited 45 times by other journals in 2015 and 35 times in 2016 – 80 citations. During those two years, the journal published in all 120 articles. The division stage yields a journal impact score of 0.67. In fact this is a not unlikely score for many social work journals.

Two preliminary points need making. First, social work journals (and many journals in the professions and social sciences generally) have far lower impact factor scores than those in science and medical journals. For example, the highly reputable *European Journal of Social Work* has at the time of writing an impact factor of 0.56.[3] This is about the same as *The American Journal of Psychology*, but a journal such as *The Lancet* has an impact factor of 44.0. Second, any citation, positive or negative, counts towards the score. In other words, any given citation may be a positive or a negative appraisal of the article. So it is not surprising that journal rankings constructed based solely on impact factors only moderately correlate with those compiled from the results of expert surveys.

There are a number of difficulties in this way of assessing the impact of published social work research. I will list them as bullet points:

- Citations tell us nothing about the impact of articles on readers rather than writers. A better figure for reader impact, albeit far from perfect, is number of downloads of specific articles.
- It takes quite some time before any new journal, however strong, can get admitted to the system. Hence, rankings reward the established journals and exclude the new.
- Research gets picked at different speeds between disciplines, such that the percentage of total citations occurring in the first two

---

[3] www.researchgate.net/journal/1369-1457_European_Journal_of_Social_Work

years after publication varies greatly among disciplines. So impact factors cannot be used to compare journals across disciplines. So it is doubtful if it is possible from such indices to know if research in, for example, sociology or education has different degrees of impact compared with research in social work.

- Impact targets push both editors and publishers to try to secure citable articles. There is a possibility that this leads, in social work at least, to pressure to publish overviews and reviews rather than original research, because the former may be cited more often.
- The strength of the relationship between impact factors of journals and the citation rates of the papers therein has been steadily decreasing. What may be happening is that some papers are getting increasingly high citation levels and thus dragging up the average for a journal as a whole. So we should not judge the quality of an individual paper or its author by the journal's impact factor.
- There is a logical circularity because the citations that count are those in journals that already are in the citation index. This seems to mean that if you have a field with a significant proportion of journals not in the index of journals, the impact factor will be distorted compared with a field where the majority of journals in the field are in the index.
- Impact factors are seductive for publishers, editors, authors, universities and perhaps funders, but not for service users, or most practitioners and managers.

The experience of doing practitioner research

In the next chapter, we spend some time sketching out the kinds of research that practitioners decide, or are persuaded, to undertake. But here our focus is different. When pursuing the chapter theme of applying research, we have placed more emphasis than usual on ways in which practice brings an agenda to research, as well as vice versa. Consistent with this, it is interesting to know how practitioners experience the process of research. I have spent some energy in collaboration with Neil Lunt and others in trying to understand and assess what is happening when practitioners engage in research.

This has brought us to the conclusion that practitioner research should perhaps be understood not as somewhere in between research and practice, nor as a combination of parts of both – but as something neither quite one nor the other. We have come to see practitioner research as a form of practice that sits creatively but uncomfortably between the established cultures of research and professional practice.

I doubt whether it is helpful to envisage practitioner research as being either 'inside' or 'outside' practice or research. The understanding that seems best to represent the experience of practitioners is to see them, in their practitioner-as-researcher work, as possessing a sociality outside, or at least on the margins of, both research *and* practice – an uncomfortable but creative marginalisation marked by an identity that is neither research nor practice.

The clearest evidence for this comes from a practitioner research initiative in Scotland between a sponsoring agency and a partnered university school of social work that was aimed at supporting practitioners to develop and undertake their own small-scale research projects. Two cohorts of practitioners were recruited.[4] Practitioners were provided with training and support to undertake a small-scale research project. Training took the form of a series of structured, face-to-face training days with ongoing one-to-one support provided by an academic tutor via contact by telephone and email throughout the research process. Teaching content was aimed at small-scale research and leaned towards qualitative rather than quantitative inquiry methods.

We were drawn to understand the data as shedding light on two orientations towards the practitioner research experience. First, the fieldwork illuminated a range of personal and relational questions of a broadly *linear* nature. For example:

- What predisposed them to become engaged in practitioner research?
- What understanding did they bring with them to their involvement and how did this understanding shift and change during their projects?
- What were the push and pull factors that led down pathways to the diverse research topics?

But also running horizontally across each of the themes were analytic ideas regarding language, memory, moral accountability, ownership, meaning, value and social work practice – we used the metaphor of weaving where you have the vertical threads and the cross-cutting weave (warp and weft are the old words used for this). It is the second of these two orientations that we touch on in the following paragraphs. We reached a number of conclusions.

---

[4] Full details about this part of the study can be followed up in Shaw and Lunt (2011, 2012). Here I simply pick illustrative extracts from the data.

1. *Practitioner researchers engage with a language and culture that is strange yet potentially rewarding for practice and research. They find themselves located in a culture that lies between 'practice' and 'research' but is fundamentally shaped by and challenges both.*

> "People speak in a different language, people use different words for different things." (Alison)[5]

> "It's something that I haven't ever done before, so to be able to talk about, undertaking a piece of research or a study in this way, I quite like that, I quite like to be learning new things and we talked before about the language, the process and that was all new to me, and then being able to see it through and I'm quite excited at this point in time about getting it written and completed and that's about a sense of achievement for me." (Shona)

2. *Practitioner researchers are typically engaged in negotiating an uncertain world, which is at its heart an effort to learn what it's about.*

Something as potentially powerful as a new culture and language will perhaps inevitably entail uncertainty. When we listen to Alison's comment that "I tried to put as much wording in of what people had actually said because I thought that's what it is about", we are hearing someone tentatively endeavouring to identify the essential nature of practitioner research. This will occasionally lead practitioners into new aspirations.

> "It's opened up a whole range of things that I've never done before and so I would like to pursue maybe ways of combining the two, if that is possible, in a more proactive way, I don't know if that's about, I don't know how even to go about that." (Shona)

This runs counter to much of the literature about practitioner research, which presents it as a slimmed-down, instrumental, novice form of research that is best tackled by learning simple rules for such inquiry. My view is that the uncertainty of practitioners is not down simply to ignorance or lack of skills, but is at least as much an endemic feature of a research practice that sits creatively but uncomfortably between the established cultures of research and professional practice.

---

[5]   All names are pseudonyms.

3. *The location of practitioner research as lying both within and outside of core professional work poses difficult challenges of moral accountability for their work within their practice cultures.*

We spoke to one person who had withdrawn from the initiative. The difficulties that were beyond her control left her saying, "It was hanging over me.... I had never failed to complete something." She was "giving myself a hard time" because "it was something I wanted to do" – something that would have been "good for me, good for the organisation". Even when at the instigation of the agency the project was closed, she said that a line had not been drawn under it: "It relieved me" but "from my point of view ... I would still want to complete that work." Jean felt bad that she was at risk of 'squandering' her opportunity. Others were scrupulously sensitive to the use of time.

4. *Involvement in practitioner research stirs reflection on the meaning and value of professional work. For some practitioners this may be overly demanding in the context of the perceived constraints of their core work.*

For a number of participants it was the strength of feeling about a project unfinished that predominated, and the sense that the wider agency programme had been foregrounded at the expense of the individual projects.

> "I really wanted something for the kids who took part in that, you know, this wasn't really necessarily something for me but it was more about the kind of process that they took part in. And that feels like that's kind of disappeared and that it has been something more *corporate*." (Focus group participant)

> "I ended up somehow presenting my research project three times to a public audience which I'm really, I am not really sure why. I kind of got into this situation where I did it at a staff conference and two other kinds of conferences and that felt like it ... it lost meaning for what it was about." (Focus group participant)

5. *The nature of practitioner research is something that emerges from the experience, rather than something that prescribes it in advance. It is only in the doing of practitioner research that its critical identity takes shape.*

I conclude with this example of the way practitioner research can, in Gillian's words, "open up so many possibilities I had not thought of".

"I think what I am and what I would like to be are different. I am a practitioner and that is my job, so that's what I have to do and I'm bound by the context of that because that is my income, that is my livelihood. I would like to be more of a researcher. It's opened up a whole range of things that I've never done before and so I would like to pursue maybe ways of combining the two."

If this is a reasonable understanding of the nature and experience of practitioner research, it raises challenges for all involved in social work, especially agency managers, the universities and practitioners.

Making practical sense

In a distinctive way, the whole of this chapter has been about making practical sense of social work research. The Cronbach material, as mentioned, would serve as useful basis for reflecting on the book theme. The brief cameos of practitioners speaking about their experience of doing research also offer a comparator. But I want to introduce some new material as a way of showing that the chapter has only begun to pose the questions.

We can find a way in to this by thinking about the broader idea of 'applied' research – of social work as part of a wider 'family' of fields of research including health, management, education, criminology, and perhaps social policy that are 'applied' – in contrast to social science fields such as sociology, much of psychology, some of economics and politics. Much of research funding in the UK at least has been shaped by this way of viewing things. Another, and also quite popular, way of reasoning is to view each of these fields as having 'pure' (or 'basic') and 'applied' 'ends'. This reflects how we think of fields like psychology and economics (as well as, of course, very different fields like mathematics). So we tend to think of basic and applied research either as two separate categories or as on a continuum, as in Figure 3.2. On this second view – disciplines as having a continuum – it is not possible to move closer to one end without moving further from the other.

Figure 3.2: The research continuum

Basic   Applied

I want to suggest two kinds of argument that question this view of things:

- First, that the pure (or basic) and applied categories, while different, are not as far apart as we are accustomed to think.
- Second, that the way we think about 'applied' has been too influenced by a rather instrumental notion of use, quality and value – one that we have questioned several times in this chapter.

In the United Kingdom in the 1990s, bridging categories like 'strategic research' were introduced to refer to research that has use in mind but not as an identifiable application or product. The expression 'purposive basic research' has the same idea in mind – pure research, but research that is done with a general application in mind, and is 'mission-oriented'. A common way of expressing such thinking is to take the single dimension pure/applied and place strategic research somewhere in the middle, as in Figure 3.3.

Figure 3.3: Strategic research

Basic ←————————————→ Applied

Strategic

While this is an improvement, it has a problem of fuzziness at the boundaries. In an important contribution to the debate, Stokes also claims that it attempts 'to force into a one-dimensional framework a conceptual problem that is inherently of higher dimension' (Stokes, 1997, p 71). Stokes was writing in *Pasteur's Quadrant*, an influential book published in 1997 by the Brookings Institution in Washington DC. He argues roughly as follows. It is possible to gain a very different view of the relationship between basic and applied research when we consider how research decisions made in some very important studies have been guided by both basic *and* applied considerations. Stokes takes Pasteur's work on microbiology. 'As Pasteur's scientific studies became progressively more fundamental, the problems he chose and the lines of inquiry he pursued became progressively more applied' (Stokes, 1997, p 13). Stokes believes we can find similar examples in the social sciences. For example, the economist Keynes 'wanted to understand the dynamics of economies at a fundamental level. But he also wanted to abolish the grinding misery of economic depression' (p 17). So Pasteur and Keynes belong not half way along but *at both ends* of the continuum in Figure 3.2.

Understanding research in this way it is likely that part of the research in any one discipline like social work should not be seen as lying on a single dimension whereby more of one means less of the other, but fully applied and fully basic.[6] 'There does not exist a category of science to which one can give the name applied science. There are sciences and the applications of science, bound together as the fruit of the tree which bears it' (as quoted in Randy Schekman's Nobel Prize speech).[7]

This immediately makes us think about the question in a different way. Instead of asking whether research is aimed at being useful *or* at gaining greater understanding and knowledge, we now ask *two* questions. Does the research have considerations of use? Does it seek fundamental understanding? We can cross the answers to yield three or possibly four kinds of research, according to what inspires the research in any given instance. In addition to Pasteur, and his work on vaccination and pasteurisation, we have Niels Bohr known for his work on atomic structure and quantum theory, and Thomas Edison, the hugely prolific American inventor.[8]

Figure 3.4: Pasteur's quadrant

		Considerations of use?	
		No	Yes
		Pure basic research (Bohr)	Use-inspired basic research (Pasteur)
Fundamental understanding	Yes	Pure basic research (Bohr)	Use-inspired basic research (Pasteur)
	No		Pure applied research (Edison)

[6] Oancea and Furlong, in a significant contribution, take exception to parts of Stokes' argument (Oancea and Furlong, 2007).

[7] www.nobelprize.org/nobel_prizes/medicine/laureates/2013/schekman-speech_en.html

[8] Can we envisage research that is led neither by concerns of use nor desire to gain fundamental understanding? Perhaps 'accidental' puzzle solving, which may fall within ideas of science as having elements of serendipity, would fall into this box. We talked about serendipity in Chapter One.

In one sense it matters little whether we think Stokes was correct. The value of his framework is that it adds to a recurring emphasis in this chapter that social work is demeaned when we think of it as a professional derivative of the ideas and theory of other disciplines.

In this chapter we have adopted a different approach to conventional discussion of research application. Rather than set out a range of examples of particular applications that may be of benefit to practice or policy, we have focused almost entirely on how best to think about the relationship between research and practice. But in what, more precisely, does social work research consist? To that question we now turn.

FOUR

Mapping social work research

This chapter opens by introducing something of what we know about the actual research that takes place in social work. I will suggest that social work research should be distinguished in terms of the primary substantive focus of the research and the primary problem focus. I will illustrate this from research by university-based researchers, service-user researchers, and practitioner researchers. I will consider differences associated with the gender of social work researchers, and then illustrate the nature of networks among both academic and practitioner researchers.

When considering what social work and associated research are essentially about, we have seen in the opening chapters that there are different ways of approaching that question. For example, we can think about it in what we may loosely call a philosophical way, by starting with what we believe to be the aims and purposes of social work and then inferring the kinds of research that would enact those purposes. My approach in this chapter is to take almost the very opposite approach, at least as a starting point. Working in an empirical way, I will set out something of what we know about the actual research that takes place. In the first part of the chapter, I will look at what we know about the content of social work research and, in general ways, what we know about the range and kinds of research methods.

Unlike the other chapters, the next few pages are more obviously data-led. Whether they tell us what we *ought* to be undertaking is a matter for the reader's appraisal in the light of wider considerations. I believe there is need for a corrective rebalancing in social work in relation to the weight we give to normative judgements, although how we describe something and the value we attach to it are never entirely separable. 'Within the description are clues to quality. A good description cannot but tell of quality' (Stake and Schwandt, 2006, p 415).

Strangely we know little about the character and content of social work research. More precisely, there have been a number of categorisations offered, too many to list here, but in general they are too rudimentary to be of great value. 'Mapping' inevitably requires some degree of simplification and reductionism. From their first beginnings, maps have been made for some particular purpose or set of purposes. The success with which the intent of the mapping is accomplished rests in the extent to which the user – in cartographic terms the percipient – understands, and is able to assess and engage with its purposes. I encountered the following delightful tale some years ago, from Lewis Carroll's *Sylvie and Bruno Concluded*:[1]

> 'That's another thing we've learned from your Nation', said Mein Herr, 'map-making. But we've carried it much further than you. What do you consider the largest map that would be really useful?' '*About six inches to the mile.*' 'Only six inches!' exclaimed Mein Herr. 'We very soon got to six yards to the mile. Then we tried a hundred yards to the mile. And then came the grandest idea of all! We actually made a map of the country, on the scale of a mile to the mile!' '*Have you used it much?*' *I enquired.* 'It has never been spread out, yet,' said Mein Herr: 'the farmers objected: they said it would cover the whole country, and shut out the sunlight! So we now use the country itself, as its own map, and I assure you it does nearly as well.'

In this chapter, we will consider the following questions:

- What is the best available way of distinguishing the kinds of research in social work?
- What do we know about the subject matter of social work research? How does this differ between university-based social work research, research by practitioners, and research where service users play a significant role?
- What can we say regarding the research methods employed in social work? How do these vary between university-based social work research, research by practitioners, and research where service users play a significant role?

There are several questions of interest that arise from this. Can we say anything helpful about possible differences in the content and methods of research from one country to another? Has social work research changed over time? We look at the first of these questions in

[1]   (Carroll, 1893, p 393)

Chapter Six, where our interest is in social work research from place to place, and the second one on Chapter Five. However, in this chapter we will say something about two further questions. Are there gender differences in the practice of social work research, and can we draw any conclusions regarding research networks in social work? As with the other chapters, we end with some reflections on making practical sense of the chapter.[2]

What do we know about the subject matter of social work research?

A scheme

We can think about this question at two different levels. First, what is the primary substantive focus of the research? Second, what is the primary problem focus of the research? To expand this second question, what is the primary orientation of the researcher to the problem, and how is the substantive issue being approached? It may be helpful to think of these two levels roughly as asking what is being done and to what end.

---

[2] I happily acknowledge the particular contributions of Alex Faulkner, Hannah Jobling, Neil Lunt, Fiona Mitchell, Matthew Norton and Anne Ramatowski to the projects on which I draw in the following paragraphs.

Figure 4.1: Primary substantive focus

Actual or potential service-user or carer groupings	1. Children, families, parents, foster carers
	2. Young people (not offenders)
	3. Young offenders/victims
	4. Adult offenders/victims
	5. Adults with housing, homelessness, education or employment difficulties
	6. People with mental health problems
	7. Older people
	8. Adults/children with health/disability difficulties (including learning disabilities)
	9. Adults/children who are drug/substance users
	10. Equal focus on two or more different user and/or carer groups
Citizen, user and community populations	11. People as members of communities
	12. Service-user, citizen or carer populations
	13. Women/men
Professional and policy communities	14. Social work practitioners /managers
	15. Social work students/practice teachers/university social work staff
	16. Social work and/or other researchers
	17. Policy, regulatory or inspection community
	18. Members or students of other occupations
	19. Jointly social work and other professional communities/agencies
Not applicable	20. For example, theorising that crosses categories; methodology

By primary substantive focus, often this will mean the people from whom data was obtained, but if it is clear that these are simply being used as 'proxies' for another set of people (for example, practitioners being interviewed to learn about children, rather than to learn about practice with children), the primary focus is on children rather than practitioners. This scheme can fairly readily be summarised through three broader grouped categories, as indicated in the left-hand column of Figure 4.1.

Figure 4.2: Primary issue or research problem

1. Understand/explain issues related to risk, vulnerability, abuse, identity, coping, challenging behaviour, separation, attachment, loss, disability or trauma.
2. Understand/explain issues related to equality, oppression, diversity, poverty, employment, housing, education and social exclusion.
3. Understand/assess/strengthen user/carer/citizen/community involvement in social work; community organisation, partnership; empowerment.
4. Understand/promote the nature and quality of informal care, carer activity, volunteering, and their relationship to formal care.
5. Describe, understand, explain or develop good practice in relation to social work beliefs, values, cultural heritage, political positions, faith, spirituality or ethics.
6. Understand/develop/assess/evaluate social work practices, methods or interventions, including their recording/documentation.
7. Understand/evaluate/strengthen social work/social care services, including voluntary/independent sector.
8. Understand/explain practice or promote good practice in social work/social care organisations, programmes and/or management.
9. Understand/respond to issues of nationhood, race, ethnicity, racism.
10. Understand/respond to issues of gender, sexism, the role of women, the role of men.
11. Understand/respond to issues about the form and significance of the family.
12. Demonstrate/assess the value of inter-disciplinary or inter-professional approaches to social work services.
13. Demonstrate/assess the value of comparative, cross-national, cross-cultural research; and of cultural distinctiveness/awareness.
14. Develop theorising.
15. Understand/appraise/develop the practice and quality of social work research (including user/carer involvement in research; uses of research, practitioner research, scientific practice, feminist research; anti-racist research methods).
16. Understand/promote learning and teaching about social work or related professions, and entry to career.

There is a general approach underlying the scheme in Figure 4.2. It aims to combine greater detail than any previous scheme, but also to avoid being overly specific. The use of different verbs (explain, understand, assess, promote, evaluate, develop) points to the numerous and often multiple intentions in any given research. These actions sometimes imply an approach to research practice – 'explain' implies a causal analysis perhaps through randomised control trial, while 'understand' may imply a hermeneutic, interpretive approach. But this is not a methods scheme for classifying.

Research content

The most detailed picture of kinds of social work research comes from a study of the *British Journal of Social Work* (*BJSW*) over a 40-year period. Most of the articles published in this journal have been written by university researchers. While a significant proportion of the articles are written from outside the UK, the journal is clearly British-led, and may not mirror research in parts of Asia, Eastern Europe or North America. But it is the fullest picture we have.

Table 4.1: Primary focus of research

	Frequency	Percentage
Children, families, parents, foster carers	45	9.3
Young people (not offenders)	9	1.9
Young offenders/victims	5	1.0
Adult offenders/victims	11	2.3
Adults with housing, homelessness, education or employment difficulties	2	0.4
People with mental health problems	6	1.2
Older people	4	0.8
Adults/children with health/disability difficulties (including learning difficulties)	9	1.9
Adults/children who are drug/substance users	1	0.2
Service-user/carer groups	92	19.0
People as members of communities	11	2.3
Service-user, citizen or carer populations	15	3.1
Women/men	12	2.5
Citizen, user and community populations	38	7.9
Social work practitioners/managers	84	17.4
Social work students/practice teachers/university social work staff	19	3.9
Social work and/or other researchers	3	0.6
Policy, regulatory or inspection community	26	5.4
Members or students of other occupations	4	0.8
Joint social work and other professional communities/agencies	37	7.7
Professional and policy communities	173	35.8
Theorising that crosses categories; methodology	180	37.3
Total	483	100.0

The research focus can be expressed more simply by grouping categories and the bold sub-totals in the table give those figures. Leaving aside the high proportion of articles that focused on more general theorising or on questions of research methodology, the most frequent empirical focus was on social work practitioners or managers. Children, families, parents and foster carers were most often the centre of attention when research concentrated on service-user or carer groups. Perhaps surprisingly, just less than one in five studies had a leading focus on service-user or carer groups. The other general conclusion these figures support is the wide spread of substantive concentrations. Social work may be no different from other fields and disciplines in this regard, but the diversity is striking.

When it comes to practitioner research the picture is rather different. Drawing on a study of practitioner research in the social care field, not surprisingly none of the research by practitioners was solely theoretical or methodological. In addition, while only 19% of the *BJSW* articles focus primarily on service-user groups, in a study of UK practitioner research the figure was 70% (Shaw et al, 2014, pp 9-10). It seems reasonable to infer that the focus for practitioner research problems is more likely to fall on issues relating to direct service delivery, and less on underlying questions of the nature, scale and experience of problems by actual or potential service users. In this respect, practitioner research probably differs from both academic research *and* user/carer research. For example, a UK-wide programme of user research in mental health – Strategies for Living – sponsored by the Mental Health Foundation[3] yielded a series of studies where the key themes at a national meeting of the grant holders for this project were centred on problems and needs as experienced by service users:

- coping;
- identity;
- information needs;
- support needs;
- self-help;
- carers;
- women's issues;
- rights and opportunities.

This limited observational evidence suggests that the 7.9% of studies looking primarily at service-user and citizen populations in the *BJSW*

---

[3] www.mentalhealth.org.uk/sites/default/files/strategies_for_living_summary.pdf

study would be much higher in user research (compare Shaw, 2012, chapter 25).

Table 4.2: Primary research problem

	Frequency	Percentage
Understand/explain issues related to risk etc.	69	14.3
Understand/explain issues related to equality etc.	37	7.7
Understand/assess/strengthen user/carer involvement etc.	12	2.5
Understand/promote the nature and quality of informal care etc.	2	0.4
Describe, understand, explain, or develop good practice in relation to social work beliefs etc.	26	5.4
Understand/develop/assess/evaluate social work practices etc.	150	31.1
Understand/evaluate/strengthen social work/social care services etc.	19	3.9
Understand/explain practice or promote good practice in social work/social care organisations etc.	21	4.3
Understand/respond to issues of nationhood etc.	3	0.6
Understand/respond to issues of gender etc.	3	0.6
Understand/respond to issues about the form and significance of the family	33	6.8
Demonstrate/assess the value of inter-disciplinary or inter-professional approaches to social work services	32	6.6
Demonstrate/assess the value of comparative research etc.	3	0.6
Develop theorising	26	5.4
Understand/appraise/develop the practice and quality of social work research etc.	21	4.3
Understand/promote learning and teaching about social work or related professions, and entry to career	26	5.4
Total	483	100.0

Turning to the question, issue or problem addressed within research (Table 4.2), again we discover that social work scholarship covers a wide range of kinds of problems and questions. However, not too far short of half the articles dealt with either understanding, developing, assessing or evaluating social work practices, or attempting to understand or explain issues related to risk.

An interesting question arises as to how far social work research topics and problems are special to social work. It seems plausible that even if there is a stable set of questions and categories that capture the identity of the field, similar sets of problems may be present in other professional and social science domains. Hence it remains an open question how far the problems and questions that preoccupy social work researchers are distinctive to the field. The risk is that members of the social work community will overestimate the distinctiveness of their contribution.

Social work research methods

Turning to the actual research methods that are employed in social work research, there is no obvious difference between the kinds of methods utilised by social workers and others in the social science field, though it is likely that the distribution will be different. Most psychologists, for example, are more likely to use measurement sales while sociologists are much less likely to deploy randomised control trials. Leaving important details of this kind to one side, Table 4.3 shows how qualitative studies outnumber quantitative ones in both practitioner and university-based research. Mixed-methods research is in a minority in both.[4]

Table 4.3: Summary of social work research methods*

	Practitioner research		BJSW articles	
Methodology	Number	Percentage†	Number	Percentage of research articles
Quantitative	18	24	91	32
Qualitative	35	47	166	57
Mixed qualitative **and quantitative methods**	17	23	32	11
Systematic reviews**	4	5	–	–
Not research	0	0	191	
Total	74		480	

Notes:
* A full breakdown of research methods can be found in the reports of these projects.
† Rounded to nearest whole percentage.
** Systematic reviews were not counted separately in the BJSW study.

[4] Mixed methods in this context means using at least one quantitative and one qualitative method. Any given quantitative or qualitative study may, of course, use multiple methods.

Bypassing more detailed questions, Table 4.3 presents a summary picture of research methods. There are two general ways in which important information is hidden in the table, first, in relation to the diversity of practitioner research, and second, with regard to gender differences in methodological choices.

Diversity of practitioner research

In the latest evidence to hand (Shaw and Lunt, forthcoming), it seems that there are different forms of practitioner research, and that using a blanket term for all instances of such inquiry may confuse rather than enlighten. We can characterise these as 'practitioner-led' and 'academic partnership' research. 'Practitioner-led' projects had a number of distinctive characteristics, one of which was that the majority had adopted qualitative methods. 'Academic partnership' projects, where practitioners had rather less autonomy, and were working in collaboration with one or more academic staff, usually in the health and medical care field, were predominantly quantitative in orientation. In this kind of practitioner research there is no difference in the balance of quantitative and qualitative studies compared with university-based practitioner researchers. In making sense of the overall differences among practitioner researchers, it seems methods choice, in ways that probably reflect established career paths in the fields of medical and health services likely that wider professional and disciplinary cultures play a predisposing role in, at least in the UK where the study took place.

Gender

The second hidden difference relates to research practices by gender. Those articles that are first-authored by women primarily in the university sphere are noticeably more likely to pursue qualitative methods than those first-authored by men.

Table 4.4: Gender of first author by methodology

			Gender of first author		Total
			Male	Female	
Research methods	Qualitative	Frequency	65	98	163
		% within research category	39.9	60.1	100
	Quantitative	Frequency	55	36	91
		% within research category	60.4	39.6	100
	Mixed methods	Frequency	12	19	31
		% within research category	38.7	61.3	100
Total		Frequency	132	153	285
		% within research category	46.3	53.7	100

The scale of the difference is considerable,[5] but its meaning and consequences are less simple. For example, there have been arguments, sometimes from within feminist science, suggesting that quantitative positions represent masculinist methodology. This is a difficult argument, partly because it explains too much. Almost two in five quantitative articles in this study were first-authored by women. Speaking of her career, Oakley says:

> I discovered that in our excitement to dismantle patriarchy I and other feminist social scientists had mistakenly thrown at least part of the baby out with the bathwater. Women and other minority groups, above all, need 'quantitative' research, because without this it is difficult to distinguish between personal experience and collective expression. Only large-scale comparative research can determine to what extent the situations of men and women are structurally differentiated. (Oakley, 1999, p 251; compare Oakley, 2014, p 258)

But the gender difference, if not everything, is quite something. These differences are reflected to some extent in the kinds of research questions and problems that women and men tackle. There are gender differences between empirically based studies and those that deal, sometimes in a more general way, with methodology and theorising.

---

[5] Tests of statistical significance were completed wherever relevant and all difference probabilities reported in this chapter were at a level of significance of at least <0.05 and in almost all cases at least <0.01.

The differences among the *BJSW* writers were fairly striking. When women were first authors, just over a quarter (26%) of the articles were focused on theorising or methodology. When men were first authors, this rose to almost a half of all articles (48%). This *may* suggest that women are more likely to write about work that involves at some stage direct focus on and perhaps contact with, people, but we should not argue this in too dogmatic a way. The cautious conclusion to draw from the findings regarding gender, research interests and methods is that the research interests of men and women *do* seem to be different, in terms of the subject and field, the questions that are brought to the field, and the methods employed. But in just what ways and for what reasons, we still know relatively little. Nor do we have any useful information about such questions when applied to research by service users or practitioners.

Networks of social work researchers

When talking about social work research in this chapter, we have assumed throughout that we have in mind single projects, whether by solo or joint authors. Picking up a theme that we touched on in the opening chapters, what do we know about networks and connections between social work researchers? David Runciman, writing in *The Guardian*,[6] captured several recurring themes in thinking about networks, technology and society: 'Networks of people with shared interests, tastes, concerns, fetishes, prejudices and fears have sprung up in limitless varieties' and 'advances in computing have thrown up fresh ways to think about what it means to own something, what it means to share something, and what it means to have a private life at all'.

Needless to say, how we think about networks – research and others – is tied closely to talk about technology. Authors considering developments in child protection have remarked that:

> [T]he 'information-age' is believed to have shifted our lives more towards the world of networks (virtual and actual) in which knowledge is defined by its utility and by its partializing, standardizing and universalizing functionality. (Pithouse et al, 2009, pp 603-4)

The general view is that these developments shape the character as well as the prevalence of networks. 'Today, dispersed collaborations

---

[6]   'Who's really driving change?', 24 May 2014.

are more feasible because communication technologies allow scientists to exchange news, data, reports, equipment, instruments, and other resources' (Cummings and Kiesler, 2005, p 704).

Unlike laboratory-based sciences, there has been little attention to the character of collaboration (or competition) between applied social scientists, or to if and in what ways research networks exist. Most of the social work articles that discuss networks are about action research or practitioner research – and not mainstream social work research. The articles that speak of networks in social work are mainly about intentionally formed networks – sometimes with a capital 'N'. There is no extended discussion of the nature of social work research networks.

To help unpick the questions that come to the fore when thinking about networks, I illustrate from two examples, one regarding a network of university-linked social work faculty, and one relating to practitioners engaged in research.

A network among university-linked social work people

This short section is based on 'snippets' from an as yet unpublished case study of a small international network comprising 15-18 people, mainly from Europe but with members from the US. Members share an interest in social work evaluation, often but not always with an institutional connection that embodies those interests. It meets somewhere in the world, usually Europe, annually. It has no formal constitution, no home site, no funding, and no external accountabilities. In these respects, it seems to be a rare instance of a classic intellectual, interest-based network. Its members had been meeting for about 18 years at the time of writing.

The network has been valued by its members. What did they regard as its nature and character? The question is complex – a "tricky question!", remarked one member. But in general people responded partly in terms of what might be called its *social disposition* (for example, mutual respect, informality, continuity) and partly in terms of its *activities* (e.g. annual meetings, annual themes, and a culture of turn taking). One person listed aspects that brought together observations made by the majority of members:

> "Its European identity matters – but ... [the US-based members] are core and influential members....
>
> The focus on evaluation in general and to some extent a 'broad church' view of evidence-based practice. So a sort of value-set....

A fairly high level of research ability in the group.... Almost all have a reputation outside the group e.g. through their research and writing....

Personal respect for one another. There has never been a high level of dissent in the group despite some differences....

Perhaps paradoxically, the fairly minimal demands the group makes on members' time, etc. Linked to this is its informality."

It often was set in contrast to more formal networks. One member made the contrast in the following way:

"What I have in mind are the kind of networks which are more formalised. For instance here in the States, the Society for Social Work and Research, National Association of Social Workers, Council on Social Work Education, are, you know, major social work organisations and they are highly formalised, they have bylaws, they have election procedures, you know, they have other things.... Cochrane Collaboration – these are, especially Cochrane, highly professionalised, formalised, and actually commercially driven network, same as the Campbell."[7]

The presence of a strong cultural dynamic seems to matter. Two of the members expressed it, in the words of one of them, as follows:

"There's a dynamic within the network which is applied versus basic if you like, or another way of putting it would be theoretically oriented versus practically oriented, and that's an important dynamic in the network, it's unresolved, and that's good, I mean it ought to be unresolved."

Someone else elaborated, suggesting that the connection between focus of interest and network culture explained why the network had continued for such a long time:

"... because in the ... exchange, the debate on evidence based practice and evaluation, we could stop in a way because ... everybody knows more or less what the members think about different topics in, in this great theme.

---

[7]   The references are to the Cochrane Collaboration and the Campbell Collaboration.

But the valuable thing is that every time somebody presents something, and (at first) maybe I think well I've heard that before, but then it makes a turn and ... [brings] a new aspect in ... to my attention, and then we have discussions on the presentations, and these are always really thought provoking. You go out after these two days and you have a lot of ideas what you could do or could read or could develop in the next month to come, every time, every year."

Another apparent sustaining element for the network was the knowingly equivocal position on whether this was a network of individuals or of institutionally linked centres. Asked if it was one or the other, one person replied:

"It is and it is not. It is built around centres but finally the persons are those who build the network.... And the network has been attractive for me over the years because of the persons and the personal relationships that allowed a very nourishing exchange."

One person illustrated the theory/practice dynamic in the following terms:

"[T]here isn't ... a way of saying that Alexis'[8] interest in Marxist social policy for example, Marxist theory, is irrelevant to the question of whether or not a 'welfare to work' possibly could work in the Netherlands. There should not be, and there never was I think in the network, a position on that, because it was clear that there were theoretical perspectives which people could offer which would inform the way in which practical application of research to policy would take place; and for me, keeping that unresolved, valuing people's theoretical contributions, without advancing theory over practical relevance was incredibly important."

Several near paradoxes seem to lie at the heart of this network, and to be part of the reason it is seen in general as a success and has proved sustainable. For example, while diverse positions may often be an *obstacle* to collaboration, in this case the opposite may have been the

[8] A pseudonym.

case. Without doubt, its very difference from networks 'with a capital "N"' that we mentioned earlier is important.

> "The Dementia Research Network and the Campbell Collaboration networks are fundamentally different. They're fundamentally organised with a single purpose – I was about to say a single *simple* purpose, but that's a bit of an overstatement – but they are bounded by a particular approach to research, a particular topic of research, whereas the virtue of [*this*] network is that it isn't."

Practitioner research

There has been a growing number of networked practitioner research initiatives. Examples can be found from Denmark, New Zealand, Scotland and elsewhere. These mainly have been practitioner-led projects. They have either been coordinated by a single agency (for example, Mitchell et al, 2010) or have drawn on practitioners from multiple agencies through a central coordinating mechanism (for example, Ramian, 2004; Lunt et al, 2008). These networked initiatives have almost always had some element of moderate funding, through direct or arm's-length government grants, to resource academic support and network infrastructure costs. They have either been one-off projects or have been organised through a series of cohorts.

The Collaborative Practitioner Research Networks Initiative (CPRN) in Denmark, started in 1998 and is perhaps the most ambitious of the three mentioned. It continues at the time of writing and has included a total of 15 networks. It has been facilitated throughout by Knud Ramian in Arhus County. Practitioners participate in a nationwide network on a common research theme and research questions. Some examples are social support for self-harm behaviour (10 studies), a follow-up on residential living (eight studies) and job retention (11 studies). The Denmark network has several distinctive features, among which is that a network consists of four to six research teams. Each team comprises at least two practitioners from an agency, who within the common theme seek to answer their own research question of concern. All research questions are developed to fit into a case-study strategy. A cross-case analysis is written at the end of each network. CPRN is managed from a regional Centre for Quality Improvement. The CPRN management provides practitioners with an initial knowledge base on each network theme, training, consultation and mentoring support in case-study methodology as the research progresses. The network organisation is funded by the ministry for social work and the agencies enter contractual agreements on timeline, seminar participation and for one working day each week for participants. Most of the reports have been in Danish, but an overview of the networking elements has been written (Lunt et al, 2012).

The practitioner initiative of CHILDREN 1st – a large voluntary agency in Scotland – and the Glasgow School of Social Work aimed at supporting individual practitioners to develop and undertake their own small-scale research projects. The project sought impact at three levels – individual, team and organisation – and two cohorts, each of six to eight practitioners, were recruited, in 2006 and 2007.

The initiative Growing Research in Practice (GRIP) in New Zealand sought to work with social service agencies to enable them to explore research questions that were of immediate concern to practitioners (Lunt et al, 2008). GRIP integrated key concepts (research support, peer support, teamwork, mentoring and partnership) into a funded programme that set a framework and timeline to achieve these outcomes. Groups of practitioners were required to conceptualise, design, undertake and disseminate their own research and the projects drew support from methods experts, mentors and peers, thus allowing groups to benchmark progress. Six workshops took place, spread over a 12-month period. The support and possible challenges that occurred were in areas such as getting started and role of support, project development and time management, and fieldwork issues and challenges. Networks differ in kind, and have different knowledge pathways.

Adapting the analysis of Edwards and colleagues (2006), practitioner research networks may include:

- New trails trodden for the first time between individual practitioners who recognise the benefits of collaborative links.
- Networks built on old networks and relationships but where there is also evidence of the influence of an innovatory ethos stemming from the research initiative.
- Old established networks that may be continued or resuscitated and operate in forms much as before but adapted for new purposes linked to practitioner research.

The networks outlined here were of the first two kinds. Their open-ended nature has the potential for mutuality and exchange. There are possible benefits for those involved in the production of practitioner research knowledge. Networks may allow for high levels of exchange to develop and be sustained during the life of the network. In the GRIP case there was also evidence of considerable loyalty being shown towards the network itself from both practitioners and mentors in order to ensure projects were completed. Furthermore, there is the potential for trust to be consolidated across network members.

However, networks are not without their challenges. Their openness may prove self-defeating. Within the network group assumptions may take root about reasons for the progress (or lack of progress) of small-scale projects. Network establishment, growth and development also entail inevitable uncertainty. For example, knowledge pathways are sometimes fluid and unstable, and networks may prove fragile. A rather different challenge stems from ambiguity regarding project ownership, and this is likely to be accentuated in those initiatives that in other respects work well and are valued by participants. In the Scotland project, this yielded a sense of individual loss and corporate transfer of ownership:

> "It's just I feel as if I've kind of gone in and done it and I go away to Edinburgh and I disappear every so often to do things like this and I come back but you know nobody's really aware of what I've done. And I kind of think that's a shame because it feels like it's been a major piece of work for me – for *me* ... I look at and I think I can't believe I actually did that but it feels like it's disappeared into the air somehow."

These difficulties notwithstanding, networks still have the potential to reap significant benefits. It will prove important to ensure a 'framework of opportunity'. The partners in the New Zealand project concluded:

> Whilst still providing ... resources during the lifetime of the project the major needs of individual projects proved to be around time management, forward planning and maintaining motivation. Although the GRIP team did indeed offer input and advice around research skills and conduct, overall our contribution is perhaps more appropriately seen as providing a framework of opportunity for projects.... Whilst at times cultural expertise is required there was – within what we call the 'framework of opportunity' – a broader sense of cultural 'permission' and affirmation being given to groups. This support allowed them to forge ahead with their work and maintain a belief that what they were doing had value. (Lunt et al, 2008, p 50)

I am aware that parts of the forgoing may paint an unduly benign picture, especially of university-based networks. The desirability of collaborative endeavour may seem to be a given, yet 'tensions and paradoxes are essential features of collaboration, even within established, co-located research groups, so the mere occurrence of face-to-face interaction does not insure that understanding and solidarity will result' (Hackett, 2005, p 668). Hackett expresses these tensions as 'openness and secrecy, cooperation and competition, priority and patience, dirigisme and autonomy, craft and articulation work, role conflicts, and risks of various sorts' (2005, p 670). Furthermore:

> Despite widespread excitement about dispersed collaboration reflected in terms like 'virtual team', 'eScience', and 'cyberinfrastructure', there appear to remain a number of challenges that scientists encounter when they work across organizational boundaries.' Thus 'technology did not overcome distance'. (Cummings and Kiesler, 2005, p 717)

Making practical sense

Recapping, we have suggested that social work research should be distinguished in terms of the primary substantive focus of the research and the primary problem focus. Among university-based researchers, we encounter a high proportion of articles that focus on more general theorising or on questions of research methodology, while the most frequent empirical focus is on social work practitioners or managers. Children, families, parents and foster carers were most often the centre of attention when research concentrated on service-user or carer groups. None of the research by practitioners was solely theoretical or methodological. Service-user researchers' attention is almost entirely addressed to problems and needs as experienced by service users. A wide range of kinds of problems and questions are brought to this research. It remains an open question how far the problems and questions that preoccupy social work researchers are distinctive to the field. Qualitative studies outnumber quantitative ones in both practitioner and university-based research, and it seems methods choices, in ways that probably reflect established career paths in the fields of medical and health services, are likely to reflect the predisposing role of wider professional and disciplinary cultures. There are significant differences associated with the gender of social work researchers. We have illustrated the nature of networks among both academic and practitioner researchers. The scheme for distinguishing kinds of research ought to be more generally adopted and where necessary modified.[9]

The diversity of topics and problems and the differences between the research concerns of university researchers, practitioners and service users may seem to support the conclusion that everyone should do what is right in their own eyes. We certainly can go as far as to say that there is no social work 'canon' of authoritative research. It sometimes is true that the social work community in a particular country may regard a person or certain books as having almost canonical status, for example, Alice Salomon in Germany and Jane Addams or perhaps Mary Richmond in the US. Being dead may be an essential qualification for inclusion, and in any case these are referencing persons rather than research.

We come back to these questions in the closing chapter. For the moment, we would caution against a council of despair. One possible implication follows from the hint above to the effect that social work research shares substantial common ground in terms of research methods with other social science disciplines and applied fields. It also shares a number of key concerns regarding the kinds of questions brought to research. That being so, inter-agency and inter-(university) departmental seminars or book/journal clubs seem one way forward.

If, on the other hand, there are important differences within social work, between practitioners, service-user researchers and those who are university-based, then planned conversations appear a strong option. The same might be said of differences within any part of the social work community. Take the case of evidence-based and 'scientific' practice. Rather than setting up barricades at one end or opting for easy abandoning of differences at the other, dialogues and exchanges that aim to understand the other and respect thoughtfully held dissenting positions would be of mutual benefit.

---

[9] User advice on implementing a slightly earlier version of the scheme can be downloaded from www.scie.org.uk/publications/reports/report17.asp.

FIVE

Social work research over time

This chapter falls near the middle of the book and is central to the arguments developed and positions taken throughout. We will work through the influence of our general worldview on how we see social work, asking the extent to which we may confidently know about our history. We will sketch out some of the current trends that feed into this. Turning our gaze to the past, we briefly demonstrate how the ways we write and speak about research have changed. We give significant space to the role of experimentation in social work. We look at the idea of the experimenting society, especially through the work of Ada Sheffield; at the success story of evidence-based practice; and at a forgotten strand of experimental sociology. We then move to consider the emergence of innovations in social work, taking task-centred social work as our main example. The ground covered in this chapter distinctively exemplifies the point made in the book's Introduction regarding the synthesis of scepticism and practicality.

When talking and thinking historically about research in social work we are inevitably influenced by our presuppositions regarding social work and its history more generally. 'Everyone knows who is traditionally said to have invented paper' – so might someone say in China. But almost no-one in Europe or the Americas knows who invented paper.[1] By extension, what we 'know' to be the most important moments in the history of social work will vary depending on whether we ask someone in Japan, Germany, Sweden, Estonia, Brazil, Egypt, Denmark, Taiwan, Italy, Australia, the UK or the US. Similar consequences would follow if we were to ask social workers from different countries what they think we should most regret or even apologise for in our histories, or if we were to ask as to the greatest characters in social work history. Indeed, what counts as social work and when it started will tell us something of what sort of stories people come to accept. A national

---

[1]   Who actually invented paper is immaterial. The point is that almost every Chinese schoolchild and almost no European or American schoolchildren will know the story of Ts'ai Lun, an official of the Imperial Court. What 'everyone knows' will usually prove a precarious assumption.

story of social work may be one of survival against political odds, or against the dominance of the 'big' nation next door, or as one's own nation exercising imperial power. In this sense, all stories of the past are really stories of the present. It may illuminate and surprise in this regard if we check out the people who appear on the History of Social Work website, developed by Jan Steyaert.[2]

Stories of this kind vary not only between nations but also over time within nations. To give just one example from my own country, even when the term 'social work' was used in something like our later sense, the make-up of the occupational mix rings strange to contemporary ears. Eileen Younghusband, when recalling her association with the London School of Economics in the mid- and late 1920s, remarked:

> I remember the whole concept of what constitutes a social worker and where a social worker should be employed was extremely vague, amorphous at that period compared with what it is now. For instance, in many quarters, personnel managers, women housing managers, youth employment bureau secretaries, were regarded as being social workers. Those were some of the employments into which social science students went. (WiseARCHIVE. The Cohen Interviews)[3]

This brings us to a recurring theme of this chapter, that the more we explore the history of social work and research, the less prone we will be to make confident generalisations. For this reason, I will spend a large part of the chapter aiming to set out a general way of thinking about and approaching the study and application of the history of social work and research. I find it hard to hit upon new ways to say something freshly settled in my mind, hence writing about the history of science and social work – one element in a more general history – I will echo arguments and indeed illustrations I have made elsewhere, although with a different audience in mind (Shaw, 2016a).[4]

We encountered ideas about the importance of being 'scientific' in social work in Chapter One. Once again this is something where ideas and assumptions have changed significantly. By and large social

[2] http://historyofsocialwork.org/eng/index.php

[3] An interesting example of how the occupational make-up of the social work community has changed over time in the US has been provided by Abbott (1995).

[4] I draw in this chapter from a more general discussion of the history of social work and science in Shaw, 2016a, chapter three.

work's predecessors a hundred years and more ago held a far more optimistic view of science than do we, although the picture is not as monolithic as often believed. In the UK, that position has often been detected in the work of the Charity Organisation Society, but it was equally evident among many who backed the Settlement movement. Take Clement Attlee – later to be one of the most significant, if least appreciated, of British prime ministers. Deeply involved in the British Settlement movement, his book, *The social worker*, repays reading on this and other things (Attlee, 1920). Scattered through his reflections, we find him saying that 'science has been rescued ... through the work of the practical social worker, the experimenter, and the investigator', such that science in this field has become 'the hopeful science', and social work 'the legacy of the prophets'. The work of science was seen as part and parcel of the work of social reform. To quote Attlee again, 'There are numbers of social workers who find in the work of research and investigation the best outlet for their desire for social service ... the scientific motive takes its place as one of the incentives that lead men to devote themselves to social service.' 'Each group of social workers, each Settlement, has been a laboratory of social science in which new theories are tested' (Attlee, 1920, pp 14-18 and 230).[5]

The science–reform nexus was connected to the influence of social evolution and British and American positivism. Evolutionary social theory was an attempt to answer not merely the question 'How does it work?', or perhaps better still, 'How does it happen?', but also 'What shall we do?' (Burrow, 1970, p 101). This general attitude to science comes through in a *Research memorandum on social work in the Depression*, first published in the 1930s, where the authors can say, almost as a given, that 'One of the great values of scientific method is in the attitude towards life that it develops. It is an attitude of confidence that encourages effort as worthwhile in itself, as well as because effort is part of an indefinite future of attainment' (Chapin and Queen, 1972 [1937], p 107).

Science, research and society

I want to give Attlee voice once more. Writing shortly after the Great War, he expressed an important distinction as elegantly as anyone when he observed that:

---

[5]   I have written more fully on this topic elsewhere (Shaw, 2014b).

Our attitude to social service will be different according to the conception that we have of society. If we regard it as at present constituted on the whole just and right, and approve of the present economic structure, social work will seem to us as it were, a work of supererogation, a praiseworthy attempt to ease the minor injustices inevitable in all systems of society. We shall see a set of disconnected problems not related to any one general question. On the other hand we may see as the root of the trouble an entirely wrong system, altogether a mistaken aim, a faulty standard of values, and we shall form in our minds more or less clearly a picture of some different system, a society organized on a new basis altogether, guided by other motives than those which operate at the present time, and we shall relate all our efforts to this point of view. (Attlee, 1920, p 10)

There are perhaps five general historical explanations of society and social change that we can distinguish. While these may seem logically mutually exclusive, such that we cannot hold more than one position at the same time, reflection on personal experience may suggest this is not so in practice. The first two are perhaps the most important and influential, and can be expressed as fall from grace versus rising from the pit. Expressed more formally, these set Romantic and Enlightenment views of history against one another. Indeed, it is possible to view much of social work's shared intellectual history and to a significant degree welfare interventions as a battle between those who wish to give emotion, spontaneity, intuition, and the life of the imagination their due recognition against those who rest their hopes in reason and the power of scientific progress.

A third position is to view history as cyclic. This is often presented as a relatively pessimistic position, as in ideas about the decline and fall of empires, and in conversational exchanges where change seen by some as progress is dismissed by others as the return of past positions and arguments. However, such a theory does not necessarily deny the possibility of social progress.[6] It is not easy to find this position expounded in the history of social work or research, though it is

---

[6] Perhaps the most important social science advocate of a social cycles view of history was Pitirim Sorokin (1889-1968) – the Russian exile who ended up at Harvard. For a recent appreciation of Sorokin's significance by Robert Benne, see www. firstthings.com/web-exclusives/2015/01/how-a-decadent-culture-makes-me-think-like-sorokin.

possibly implicit in various arguments. For example, Davies' debated and significant argument about social work as often involving 'maintenance' (see, for example, Davies, 2013) certainly seems to move away from a linear model of social work. Davies would place his position within the merits of systems theory and Mertonian functionalism for justifying the existence of social work: 'I remain of the view that the underlying dynamic is concerned with the security of society, the social survival (or maintenance) of people deemed to be at risk and the provision of new opportunities for individuals to regain the initiative to further their own welfare.'[7]

History as relativising, a fourth general position, can be seen in some forms of postmodernism, in the critical, post-structural interpretivism adopted by the well-known sociologist Norman Denzin, and in the development of a strong paradigm position with its idea of the incommensurability of knowledge between paradigms. While this is not expressed as a view of the history of research, it denies the possibility of any linear view of progress, or perhaps of decline.

Finally, there are views of history as in one way or another the exercise of power. This is evident, for example, in German critical theory and some parts of its heirs in European social theory, and in Foucault's work, where 'Power is not something that simply forbids and represses, but is something that produces particular kinds of knowledge' (O'Farrell, 2005, p 45). We can see this when history is explained as the story told by the winners. To give just one example, the historian of sociology, Jennifer Platt, complains that:

> Accounts written from within sociology, as history of sociology, generally treat both other disciplines and groups outside the academy as parts of the background. They are seen as instrumental to the main aims of sociologists, or as introducing distortions into the ... course of pure sociological development. (Platt, 1996, p 264)

She has social work in mind here. The work of Jane Addams and the Hull-House Settlement in Chicago is a case in point. The Hull-House

---

[7] Personal communication, 21 August 2014. Davies' position can be connected in this respect to that of Perlman when she grumbled about 'the caseworker's aspiration (rarely his client's) to goals that are illusory: achieving "cure" for instance, rather than the more realistic goal of achieving some restored or new equilibrium' (in her Foreword to Reid and Shyne, 1969, p vi).

Settlement was collecting systematic data before the University of Chicago's sociology department was founded.

> ... those methods and indeed topics, which were characteristic of the 'Chicago School' were equally characteristic of social workers and voluntary activists who were in the field somewhat sooner. (Platt, 1996, p 263)

Task Box 5.1: 'My' history of social work

Which of these ways of explaining the history of social work do you find attractive? Why do you think you are drawn to some rather than others? Are there ways your underlying assumptions shape and sometimes limit how you see the history of social work and research in your country?

Can we detect what is happening?

If readers were to pause at this moment and spend 10 minutes listing what they believe to be the more important wider trends that are shaping social work and its associated research, the chances of agreement – between them or indeed with me – are slight. But endeavouring to gain a perspective from at least middle distance is worth the effort, so here goes. I offer these in no special order nor with any approval ratings, for I am not an enthusiast for either the Romantic or Enlightenment world views. I neither lament that things are not what they used to be, nor look for a yet brighter future.

The dominance of the US has to be taken into account. This has various aspects. It is partly a question of the academic ascendancy of the English language. Even in countries where the research ethos of US social work research may not be shared, there is a pressure to publish in English, and the main reference sources for practitioners always include some that are written in or directly echo those in English.

It is not immediately obvious what constitutes the distinctive elements of the nature and character of US social work scholarship. I think there is a collective self-containment in US work. This can be seen, for example, in the way that journal articles by US writers rarely cite any work by those beyond its shores.[8] It is possible also that the location of social work in free-standing 'schools' within American

---

[8]   I have offered, briefly, some evidence about this elsewhere (Shaw, 2014a).

universities reinforces this self-containment.[9] There also is an apparent wish to be seen as having scientific qualities and discipline status.

The dominance of English-language work means that often approaches are filtered through a US lens. Take approaches to research methods. Flick, for example, contrasts the development of qualitative research methods in the US and Germany when he concludes:

> In Germany we find increasing methodological consolidation complemented by a concentration on procedural questions in a growing research practice. In the United States, on the other hand, recent developments are characterized by a trend to question the apparent certainties provided by methods. (Flick, 2006, p 19)

The influence of US research has spread to other countries – parts of Eastern Europe, for instance, Canada, Israel and parts of Asia (such as Hong Kong, Singapore, South Korea). One mechanism for this seems to be the numbers of scholars from those countries who complete their PhDs in the US.

The rise of evidence-based practice probably has claim to inclusion in this middle-distance survey. I return to this as a more detailed case example later in the chapter, for evidence-based practice certainly has a success story to tell.

Specialisation represents a more general characteristic and trend that we can trace back for at least a century. Social work finds its research home in a university world where differentiation and specialisation have continued since the late 19th century. As early as 1919, Max Weber, when speaking to graduate students in Germany, referred to the 'much talked-about' issue of how 'science has entered a phase of specialization previously unknown' (Weber, 1948 [1919], p 134), and how the individual achieves by being 'a strict specialist'. Stephen Fuller refers to 'the increased disciplinization of the scaled-up modern university' where the autonomy of inquiry is 'relativized to particular disciplines' (Fuller, 2009, p 23). I do not have figures, but I think we can safely say that there has been a great expansion in the number of social work journals. I wonder also if we can see an elaboration and differentiation of research methods.

---

[9] The establishment of free-standing schools also can be viewed as the consequence rather than effect of a desire for an independent identity. I suspect that both are at work.

Social work, both practice and research, are marked by **credentialism**, where publically available national grades and rankings are now commonplace, and where for universities these sometimes are international. Within the university world, we also should include the growth in the number of social work doctoral programmes.

Linked to the growth of credentialism, we considered the demand for **research impact** in Chapter Three, in part through the growth of research metrics, such as journal impact scores, and in part via the demand of governments for research that has 'impact'.

In the previous chapter, we also asked whether we are witnessing **growing networks and collaboration**, wondering whether the ready availability of social and communication media has increased the opportunities for such networking and collaboration. We have seen that this is a complex question, and one on which we may be reluctant to express firm views.

In the following part of this chapter, I will turn to a series of more particular questions:

• How has the idea of doing an experiment developed in social work?
• How do we account for the success of evidence-based practice?
• Is it possible to understand the nature and emergence of what we come to regard as 'innovations' in social work and research?

I will turn, as with other chapters, to the questions this raises about making practical sense of the chapter. But before embarking on these questions, I will note briefly the fairly marked ways in which styles of academic writing about social work have changed over time. This part of the chapter is intended to unsettle those assumptions about standard ways of writing that social workers encounter and imbibe within social work training programmes and thereafter.

Writing social work

The best evidence to hand comes from the study of the *British Journal of Social Work (BJSW)* referred to in the previous chapter. At the time of this study, the journal had published more than 2,000 articles over its history. How were they written? Had there been trends and changes over the time of the journal's history? It is helpful to compare the journal with how scholarly work has been reflected in the journal that stood as its nearest predecessor, the quarterly *Social Work*. *Social Work* reflected a journal culture quite different from what was to follow – far less proceduralised, and suggesting a level of editorial power and discretion. As one early editor of the *BJSW* who had written for that previous journal recalled, 'If the editor liked the submission then it would be likely to be published and they consulted other people at their discretion rather than a very formalised system of peer review.'

Few of the referencing details that now would be regarded as standard (journal page numbers or parts, author initials, book publishers, place of publication, and consistency in how authors are listed) were so regarded in 1970. Second, there was a strong US-directed gaze in a significant proportion of the articles, more so than would now be expected. Almost every reference was either to British or American literature. Third, there was a language of respectfulness, the tone of which was carried through to how men and women were referred to in the journal. However, the practice of often giving first names of authors made gender more visible than is often the case in 21st-century social work journal writing. Fourth, earlier writing conveys an immediacy. In the correspondence columns, almost all the letters were published in the issue immediately following the one in which the article commented on had appeared. There is a sense of exchange and immediacy that is rarely found in later journals, even in online journals. The journals obviously had a much quicker turnaround than our later, more technologically equipped, age can manage.

When we examine the representation of scientific method, while the proportion of research-based articles is not that different from contemporary social work journals, there is little reflection on the research process. Nothing is said about how data were analysed, and no awareness of methodological writing appears in the journal. Influential methods texts were just appearing by writers such as Norman Denzin and Aaron Cicourel, but would not influence social work for a few years.

The shifts that took place in the decades ahead were part of a process of academisation, in the sense that the subject was becoming increasingly 'academic' and was developing a research culture, with consequent pressure to develop curricula embedded in research. There is a further meaning to 'becoming academic' that carries the association of cultivating a scepticism in stance. We should not interpret these differences and changes as evidence of social work becoming stronger in its scholarly work – though this was almost universally the way former editors viewed their journal:

> 'The standards expected of those who write for the journal have increased steadily in terms of we want papers that are well researched, rigorously referenced, and topical, new, original. So I mean in that sense the goal posts have steadily

moved towards better quality papers ... when you compare what's published now and what was published 40 years ago, yes, a remarkable change in style, quality, I think in all ways'

The reason for sketching the outlines of writing practice is to prompt reflective questioning regarding how conventions often taken as given are rather the customs and social habits currently given authority.

Task Box 5.2: How writing style conveys messages

Taking either a research article you have published or one by a writer whose work you value, what are the important hallmarks of the writing style? What 'messages' do they convey to the reader?

The experimenting social worker

We remarked earlier when discussing the general beliefs and assumptions that people bring to understanding historical change how social work's shared intellectual history and to a significant degree welfare interventions can be viewed as a battle between those who wish to give emotion, spontaneity, intuition, and the life of the imagination their due recognition against those who rest their hopes in reason and the power of scientific progress. We first encountered this in Chapter Two where we considered the values, tensions, checks and balances that follow from seeing the purposes of social work research as being to pursue evidence, understanding and justice. We have seen also how social workers' responses, while they may have a common core, ebb and flow over time in regard to the relative levels of confidence in the power of science. In what follows, I will endeavour to put flesh on the bones of this argument. This entails three general points.

- The idea of experimenting as part of welfare practice has been central to the positions of those from different 'traditions'.
- I will come closer to the present to pick up a point made already, that evidence-based practice has a success story to tell, and to ask what may be the elements of that story.
- I will then step back again in time to outline an almost entirely forgotten story of how experimental research designs of a particular kind once had an active presence in a discipline that now gives little or no attention whatever to the question – sociology.

The first and third points draw largely on sociology in the US, while the second one offers a cross-national and cross-discipline story. I should stress that in none of these arguments am I simply trying to fill in historical gaps for the sake of prosaic accuracy or completeness. My concerns are twofold – to act on my assumption that social work has much to gain from the preoccupations it shares with other disciplines, and to accentuate the richness, density and involvedness that are entailed in social workers' commitment to good evidence.

Experimenting in Chicago and Boston

'The marginal status of experiment in sociology ... goes back to the duality between the natural sciences and the human sciences in the German tradition of idealistic philosophy' (Gross, 2010, p 175), of *Naturwissenschaft* and *Geisteswissenschaft*. Nonetheless, Robert Park and some of his Chicago colleagues spoke of the notion of a self-experimenting society, and the concepts of 'laboratory' and 'experiment'. Albion Small, the first head of the sociology department at the University of Chicago, insisted 'All life is experimentation. Every spontaneous or voluntary association is an experiment. Every conscious or unconscious acquiescence in a habit is an experiment' (Small, 1921, p 187). Park not only saw experiments as taking place in society but 'even more important – as performed by society itself' (Gross, 2010, p 181). Also 'the Chicagoan approach to viewing settlements as social laboratories places the sociological experimenter right in the middle of experimental practices' such that 'they saw the laboratory experiment as a special case of the general or the "real" experiment in society – and not vice versa' (p 182). The idea was familiar more generally. In Chicago, in addition to Park, Ernest Burgess, Clifford Shaw and Henry McKay – names famous in the history of sociology – all spoke of their work in such terms. In the UK, Clement Attlee, later prime minister, writing of British settlements, described them as 'social laboratories, where new ideas can be worked out and experiments tried of every variety of new social effort' (Attlee, 1920, pp 215-16).

A ready extension of this point can be made by noticing an aspect of the arguments of the largely forgotten sociological social worker, Ada Sheffield,[10] and how she tied a socially contextualised view of social work to endeavours to reach causal explanations. The way Sheffield thought about cases is reflected in her criteria when she asks

---

[10] For an introduction to the life of Ada Eliot Sheffield, largely through her correspondence with her brother T.S. Eliot, see Shaw (forthcoming).

'What is "success" in case work?' and 'Just what is the case worker's "case"?' Sheffield sees a case as the network of interested people ('a whole complex web of persons and circumstances', Sheffield, 1937, p 75) and as possessing a temporal continuance. Hence the worker 'is intellectually in need of a *unit of attention*' (p 76) – a focus of concerns. She criticises trends in American social work over the previous decade for their individualising focus. For Sheffield it is the 'situation' that is the unit of attention, rather than the individual – 'a definite web of elements, current and past, that reveal and explain his present need in its wider bearings' (p 78). She talks of how this makes social work 'less client-centered' and how the 'unit of treatment has become a dynamic field of experience, a field in which the individual or the family figures within an aggregate of interactive and inter-dependent factors of personality and circumstances' (p 78).

Seeing things as 'situation-units' for Sheffield 'represents a way of viewing a "case"' and brings into focus 'things which it helps the worker to see' (p 79). She see the case situation as having four aspects – fact content, scope, a 'pattern' and process. Among the innumerable possible facts, it is for her social purpose that decides their relevance, and she sets this against the risk that the case worker's 'vision may catch only items that fall in with conventional and uncritical interpretations' (p 81). 'Many items, *imaginably relevant*, are not actually so *thought* unless they can be seen as figuring in a cooperatively directed social process' (p 81; emphasis in original). She spoke more specifically about what she had in mind in her earlier book where she expounded the principle that '[i]nterpretation of diagnosis is the discovery of cause-effect relations among fact-items which taken separately are without any relevance to any purpose' (Sheffield, 1922, p 40) and insisted that each fact-item is not discrete but 'knit together in a causally relevant network', such that, in a delightful turn of phrase, other fact-items 'cling to it' (p 55). She had a note that groupings of fact-items 'get their meaning ... not only from the cause-effect relation among their respective fact-items but also from a felt relation between these meanings and the whole course of the case history' (p 57) – the remoter causes and effects.

The scope – 'how far out we must look' (Sheffield, 1937, p 81) – comprises 'the cultural and institutional setting of our common life' (p 82) over time. This has a 'pattern' – 'the way its distinctive factors are organized' (p 80). Identifying a pattern that is relatively constant 'should clarify causative relations, should help us to follow social process, and to raise significant questions' (p 91-92).

This brief foray tells us several things. The Chicagoan sociologists and those social workers who found kinship with them placed emphasis on the importance of context, in ways that led in a different research direction from the early quantitative and statistical sociology that was emerging at places like Columbia University.[11] This approach enabled participants to ascertain, or at least focus on, the causes of things. The contemporary relevance of this historical aside is increased because there were important connections and affinities between social work and sociology, even when personal and departmental interests kept the two apart. Including Ada Sheffield in the argument – someone of whom the leading sociologist Ernest Burgess appreciatively remarked 'with her theoretic statement I find myself in complete agreement' (Burgess, 1928, p 526) – makes exactly this point.[12] In addition, a case can be made for saying that the commitment to survey methods and quantitative approaches in the early social work programme at Chicago had rhetorical purposes different to those of Sheffield, to set out a scientific basis for distinguishing the social work field.[13]

The successful invention of evidence-based practice

Is evidence-based practice something we have discovered or invented? Was it something waiting to be found once we had the means by which to do so? Or have we used certain tools to craft a way of doing things? Have we *excavated* evidence-based practice or *fashioned* it? Here is an apparently historical argument about evidence-based practice:

> The first shift in social work, from a morally based to an authority-based practice paradigm, was finalized by the early 1930s. The second shift, which is an attempt to transition from an authority-based to an empirically based practice paradigm, was initiated in the late 1960s and 1970s but has not been completed. (Okpych and Yu, 2014, p 5)

---

[11] This is almost a gross simplification but adequate to support the main point about the foundations of experimentation.

[12] Interested readers can pursue this in the literature. I have written about it in some detail (Shaw, 2009, 2016b), and the earlier history of sociological research in the US by the British sociologist Jennifer Platt (1996) makes the point in various ways, as does Ray Lee in his important paper on the history of the interview (Lee, forthcoming).

[13] However, the *actual* methods employed may have been closer to those going on across the Chicago campus among the sociology faculty and doctoral community than either set of participants was able to acknowledge (compare Shaw, 2015a).

The key terms are the expressions 'morally based', 'authority-based' and 'empirically based'. It will be clear that this is a helpfully unambiguous example of an Enlightenment view of history, with its faith in the power of scientific progress. Indeed, these key terms are almost identical in meaning to those of Auguste Comte, the advocate of first-generation positivism and the coiner of the term 'sociology', who argued that society proceeds through theological, metaphysical and positive phases, although we should note the caveat – 'but has not been completed' – that we often find in similar statements. For these authors, evidence-based practice represents an unbiased way of learning about the world to which we all should aspire.

One difficulty with this position is that, while it seems to be a historical argument, it brings a prior historical scheme through which the 'unhelpful' influences of morality and authority are filtered out of science. As it happens, Sackett's classic definition of evidence-based practice expresses it rather differently as 'the conscientious, explicit and judicious use of current best evidence in making decisions about the care of individual patients' (Sackett et al, 1996, p 71). This entails three kinds of claim: **moral** ('conscientious' claim); **wisdom** ('judicious' claim) and **transparency and openness** ('explicit' claim). A second difficulty is that it this definition fails to recognise the historical and social factors that support and sustain the success of evidence-based practice. These factors suggest that we should more helpfully think of evidence-based practice as an invention, as the creation of our times, rather than a discovery. Evidence-based practice has successfully held sway for numerous reasons:[14]

- It offers a link to medicine through the key definition by Sackett and colleagues and therefore offers borrowed professional status.
- It is readily transferable to and from various fields of applied study (for example, criminology, education, health, social work), so has become embedded within a bigger picture larger than any one field.
- It can produce programme packages that can be sold on to agencies. 'What works?' seems to have commercial value. Collins and Pinch remark in a different context that 'Commercial standards of proof can run in a very different direction to scientific standards' (1998, p 88).
- It has strategic and methodological affinities with the work of the Cochrane and Campbell Collaborations, which gives it an infrastructure for development and diffusion.

[14] I have made this argument previously (for example, in Shaw, 2016a) but as it feels plausible, I repeat it here.

- It seems to offer a bridge between academic and 'applied' work and promises a way to avoid theory–practice tensions. It thus has the potential to interest policy and practice fields.
- It is capable of varied interpretations and applications, so captures a number of issues. It takes on the flexibility – and imprecision – of what Karl Popper termed a 'bucket' category.
- It links readily to related discourses such as the advocacy of the need for 'scientific practice' in American social work.
- It is offered by its advocates as atheoretical, so requiring less intellectual sophistication to grasp the basic motifs. As a consequence, it is more easily taught on social work and professional programmes.
- It seems to travel well through time (a rhetorically plausible case can be made for historical pedigree from as early as the Charity Organization movement in the late 19th and early 20th centuries, the work of American social work pioneer Mary Richmond around the same time, and the 1960s 'What works?' debates in the field of offending, for example McGuire, 1995) and place (it is presented as culture-free).
- Its limitations of argument are clear, so it invites those 'outside' to react to it by way of 'correction' and thus stay within the frame of reference.

To repeat, I am not introducing evidence-based practice into this chapter to assess whether or not it is 'true' or 'valid', but to understand it as part of the history of social work that has gained success through a powerful mix of social, intellectual and rhetorical elements.

Task Box 5.3: Thinking about intervention

Bring to mind a model of social work intervention that you esteem highly. What 'strengths' do you think this model has apart from evidential ones? These may be social, philosophical or rhetorical.

Experimental sociology

We now turn to the third of our observations related to seeing social work as about experimenting in one way or another – that experimental research designs of a particular kind had an active presence in sociology for a period of almost 40 years between the second and sixth decades of the last century, if almost wholly in the US. As Platt (1996) notes, many of the substantive concerns of this research strand shared kinship with social work.

Writing in 1945, Ernest Greenwood observed that 'During the last twenty years much has been written in social science periodicals about the possibilities and impossibilities of an experimental sociology' (p 5). The main figures in this field were Stuart Chapin and Greenwood himself. The most settled and complete accounts of their work can be found in books they each wrote towards the end of their careers (Chapin, 1955 [1947]; Greenwood, 1945), but Chapin in particular was a prolific contributor to the journals. They distinguish between and deal with naturally occurring and created or artificial experiments, and it is the former for which their work remains significant. The *ex post facto* or natural experiment entails the researcher being able to 'imagine the experiment in his [sic] mind' (Greenwood, 1945, p 13). It can be thought of as an experiment in reverse, seeking to infer back to causes from observed effects, rather than the model of, for example, a randomised control trial, inferring from cause to effect.

Studies were undertaken on topics such as the relationship between school performance, extracurricular activities or involvement in community groups and subsequent economic or social achievement; and the mental, physical and environmental antecedents of delinquency. The ethical difficulties associated in social work with many possible applications of randomised experimentation give such designs continuing interest and attraction.

An assessment of their work would take us into detailed and sometimes technical considerations. But we can gain a general understanding by starting with Chapin's often-made point that 'Experimental sociology is that study of sociological phenomena which proceeds by making observations under conditions of control' (Chapin, 1932). So with Greenwood, 'Effective control is the key to the entire experimental procedure.... Without proper control we cannot be certain that the causal nexus which we seek to establish is a real one' (1945, p 72).

The centrality of the question of control stems from the demands of starting from observed 'effects' and seeking to manipulate the data to enable a plausible inference backwards about the likely causes. Greenwood remarks that 'when we try to decipher what is really meant when we say that causes produce their effects, we encounter difficulties' (1945). For example, we may start from the classic argument that it requires temporal succession – but often 'our notion of what comes first and last is governed by our position in relation to the phenomenon, that is, by our frame of reference' such that often 'much reciprocity goes on between the so-called cause and effect' (p 20).

I have made this brief reference to a central question only in order to show what we can learn from how Chapin and Greenwood endeavoured to resolve it. Before doing so, we should place Chapin and Greenwood in the wider stream of thought. Martindale distinguishes between pluralistic behaviourists (such as Chapin and Greenwood), symbolic interactionists, and social-action theorists, but explains the underlying coherence in how these different groups theorised methodology.

> (1) They sought a definition of sociological subject matter in terms of idealistic theories; (2) they avoided as far as possible the assumption of large-scale social units … as units of sociological analysis; they were, in one terminology, strongly "nominalistic"; (3) they had as one foremost problem the development of a theory of social persons; and (4) they brought the problem of sociological method under review. (Martindale, 1961, p 303)

In other words, we have advocates of experimentation that worked within a very different frame of reference from today's practitioners of randomised control trials. Greenwood, for example, pays his dues to early sociologists such as Charles Cooley and William Sumner. He also acknowledges Albion Small, Herbert Mead, Pitirim Sorokin, Robert Park, Robert Lynd, W.S. Robinson, Florian Znaniecki, Dorothy Thomas, Robert MacIver and Vivian Palmer, Paul Lazarsfeld and Stuart Chapin. Within Greenwood's text we find also Weber, W.I. Thomas, Margaret Mead and Frederick Thrasher. While some of these names will not be familiar to present day readers, it suffices to say that many are writers who normally are treated as occupying positions oppositional to those of present day proponents of experimental designs.

Take for example, Chapin's remarks as president of the American Sociological Association:

> Techniques are no more effective in the long run than the soundness of the basic logic that underlies them. Technique should not become an end in itself lest you remain a skilled artisan instead of a creative worker who invents and discovers. Technique should not become a snobbish escape device in which you seek mere intellectual security. Do not fear intuitive insights which may lead to fruitful new hypotheses. Remember that social values are an important subject matter of study and value judgments contribute

to decisions on what to study. But try to keep your value systems from undermining the objectivity of your research method. ('Presidential Advice', 1953, p 599)

How might such 'intuitive insight' operate? Greenwood spells it out in the following way. A judgment is needed as to the relevant factors to control. Greenwood picks up the suggestion from Max Weber that we can think away factors that we can judge from experience are not relevant. Greenwood calls this 'identifying relevance through insight' (Greenwood, 1945, p 74) and calls it 'a prescription not easy to fill' (p 74).

> The efficient and successful utilization of the experimental method depends upon a rather complete knowledge of the materials to which that method is applied. Whatever names we may prefer to call it – insight, understanding, or what not – such preliminary acquaintance is imperative. (p 74)

More generally, 'the experiment succeeds if it is based on good insight, and it fails if it is based upon false insight' (p 74). For social phenomena, the investigator can observe cause because 'he [sic] has at his disposal the added instrument of *Verstehen*. He can always check the behaviour of others in himself' (p 21).

It falls outside the scope of this book to enquire after the reasons for the demise of experimental sociology, although the influence of Donald Campbell was no doubt a significant factor. Campbell dismissed Greenwood and Chapin almost out of hand in terms of threats to validity, concluding 'the sociological tradition of "ex post facto" designs ... is totally rejected' (Campbell and Russo, 1999, p 81). Yet the disappearance of this tradition illustrates how one area of potentially fruitful exchange between sociology and social work was lost, and with it one potential avenue for critical exchange of ideas and practices between researchers who usually stay on opposite sides of various fences.

Innovations in social work research

Before we briefly reflect on ideas for making practical sense of this chapter, we glance at the question of if and how innovations are introduced into social work over time. Ian McEwan speaks of a character in his novel *Amsterdam*, a musician, in ways that capture something of innovation. 'Each day he made attempts ... but produced nothing but quotations, thinly or well disguised, of his own work. Nothing sprang free of its own idiom, its own authority, to offer the element of surprise that would be the guarantee of originality' (McEwan, 1998, p 61).

Xenitidou and Gilbert (2009) developed a definition of innovation and applied that definition to a sample of research articles. Wiles and colleagues (2009) conducted a narrative review of qualitative research published between 2000 and 2009 in which the authors *made claims* to methodological innovation. Wiles and colleagues observed that authors rarely defined what they meant by innovation. Closer analysis of 'innovation' at the highest level of new inceptions revealed over-claiming, and there was little evidence of paradigmatic developments within qualitative research methods. The majority of the innovations involved the altering of existing methodological traditions. Interestingly, there was almost no duplication between the studies *judged* to be innovative by Xenitidou and Gilbert, and those *claimed* to be innovative by the authors reviewed in Wiles et al's study.

What are the conditions for innovation? Nind (2015) suggests that the primary conditions are as follows:

• dissatisfaction with existing methods or approaches;
• identification of new phenomena;
• opportunity to develop something new;
• innovation that must address either individual or social science 'need';
• innovation that must be feasible/workable/accessible.

I believe that research innovation may be more likely to occur when there is a deep and collective, though coincidental, sense of a problem, a network of able and creative researchers, and a degree of intellectual and experimental tension. But can we plan for this? We considered in Chapter One ways in which we should think of the ideal balance between planned and unplanned research or practice interventions through the work of Merton and Barber where they plead for the absence of rigid control over the work of scientists. They were arguing for 'planning in general with indefiniteness as to specific problems' (2004, p 144), because 'compulsive tidiness' keeps the scientist from being open to fruitful surprises. This pushes to the fore questions of the ideal organisation of social work research, for example where resources should be concentrated. I also believe that research innovation will be more fully accomplished inasmuch as it recognises local knowledge and expertise; is conveyed through both planned and informal facilitator roles; acknowledges the various influences of existing and new networks; promotes social work inquiry marked by rigour, range, variety, depth and progression; sustains an active conversation with the social science community; and harnesses opportunities for organisational discretion and change.

We can anchor this discussion by talking the example of task-centred intervention, associated with the work of William Reid.[15] What gave it success as an intervention? There are some resonances here with our remarks about the success story of evidence-based practice. First, it could plausibly claim to have both continuity with previous valued practice positions, while offering a significant break – to trust the tradition, while at the same time claiming an independent position from which this tradition may be reinterpreted. Fortune observes that 'most practitioners could find some aspect of the task-centered model that was similar to what they were already doing, and this familiarity tempered some of the perceptions of how radical the model was' (Fortune, 2012, p 24). Among its hallmarks, she describes it as an 'intermediate approach' (p 31) that enabled practitioners to change without having to sign up to something that seemed an abandonment of existing valued positions.

Second, it fitted into wider influential narratives, without seeming a mere sub-category of something bigger. Fortune, in her role as 'threshold guardian', argues that the model belongs to the family of evidence-driven and linear intervention models while being distinctively American, unlike the British import of evidence-based practice (Fortune, 2014). 'It has consistently modelled an empirical orientation to practice' (Rooney, 2010, p 198). Rooney makes an interesting remark in this context regarding how task-centred practice has proved itself as a 'metamodel for how social work models or approaches could be constructed'.

Task-centred practice gained strength, third, by virtue of being able to bolt on otherwise unconnected discourses that were at most on the margins of Reid's own technological frame. In the late 1960s and early 1970s, for example, there were emerging concerns that social work practice almost routinely disregarded or explained away the views of the client. While there is little evidence to align Reid with broader

---

[15] An authoritative introduction to the model can be read in the National Association of Social Workers and Oxford University Press *Encyclopedia of social work* at http://socialwork.oxfordre.com/view/10.1093/acrefore/9780199975839.001.0001/acrefore-9780199975839-e-388. I have written more fully on task-centred social work and inventions in social work elsewhere (Shaw, 2016a).

movements of this nature, it was significant that task-centred practice could be promoted as 'the first social work practice model to focus on the *client's* actions' (Videka and Blackburn, 2010, p 188; emphasis in original).

The dimension of reciprocal work tasks for social worker and client also implied a practice value enabling commentators to make the rhetorical assertions that it 'has embodied the social work value of self-determination and supported client empowerment and facilitating strengths' (Rooney, 2010, p 198), and 'was client centred and client driven even before empowerment and strengths-based practice became the mantra of the profession' (Videka and Blackburn, 2010, p 188).

Making practical sense

Having read this far, then, the main thrust of the chapter will have gained some purchase – to set out a general way of thinking about and approaching the study and application of the history of social work and research. The assertion that the more we explore the history of social work and research, the less prone we will be to make confident generalisations may seem more plausible. All of the areas we have touched on in this chapter – the influence of our general worldview on how we see social work, the extent to which we may confidently know about our history, doing experiments, making innovations, the ways in which influential frames of reference for social work are embedded in social and historical contingencies – come within this rubric.

We may also come to doubt how radically different the future will appear from the present, though we are on still less certain ground. I suspect that some elements will continue. For example, evidence-based practice, or at least the questions for which it stands, will continue to both challenge and fracture how the priorities for gaining understanding should be set. I endorse the elegant remark of a colleague when he valued an organisation culture he had been part of in the past where "reasoned heresy was preferred to unthinking orthodoxy".[16] Likewise with qualitative and quantitative methods and what such questions stand for. For example, we will hear more about 'big data', arising from continued increases in computational power. I suspect there will be a revival of quantitative research in social work. 'Wars and rumours of wars' will exercise perhaps a more pervasive challenge for both practice and research, as may the agenda arising from the emergence of certain faith-based approaches to social work. The

---

[16] With acknowledgement to Dr Jonathan Evans.

difficulty of confident generalisation stems in part from differentiating the global and the local. It is to such questions of place that we turn in the next chapter.

SIX

Place and space

Continuing with the approach in Chapter Five, this chapter begins with ways in which awareness of the meaning and importance of place is shared between the humanities and social work. Moving on to a consideration of that over-familiar term globalisation, this leads on to a more general consideration of how research practices occur in space and place. This book is not where one would think of turning for discovering and applying research methods. But when we consider how social work and research take place from place to place, and in spatial contexts, then some of the clearest illumination can be shed on this question by research methods, perhaps especially those that we would think of as qualitative in nature. Much of the later part of the chapter is given over to how research methodology addresses questions of place and space. We conclude with briefer than usual suggestions about making practical sense of the chapter.

Social work research takes place within temporal, social, relational, cultural, faith, governmental, political, institutional, ethical, intellectual, spatial and practice contexts. At any given period, there usually will be sufficient common understanding and acceptance of the purposes of social work research to enable the social work community across different nations and cultures to engage in near-enough mutual understandings and practices. However, the character, purposeful priorities and uses of social work research will always be shaped – diversely – by the challenges of the places in which it occurs.

What are our assumptions of the meaning of 'social work context'? Possibly roughly the same as 'setting' or 'agency' and as something that is a 'given' of social work practice. Something we can 'touch, taste and handle' – that is relatively fixed and durable – social work's material culture. Maybe we distinguish in our minds the local from the extended setting. This extended setting may be spatial, or defined by membership. Service users may well appear in our image of the social work context, or the domains of nation, community, health and so on. In all of this, 'time' and 'place' are high-level concepts by which we structure and make sense of the world, and 'use effortlessly all the time ... yet are quite unable to define' (Fulford and Columbo,

2004, p 131). As we approach these issues, the underlying assumption of this chapter is rather similar to that of Chapter Five. Distance or closeness of place and space raise comparable questions to those of time-closeness or distance.

But by way of preamble, and with the aim of steering a course away from social work provincialism, we will open out the theme by recognising that when embarking on considerations of place in social work and research, we ought not to imagine we have something to say that speaks only in a social work voice. Memory and time, place and space act as stage and staging posts on and towards which the meanings of our lives are played out. The particular and the universal are in constant interplay. Creative writers have been particularly attuned to this. It was Patrick Kavanagh, the Irish poet, who wrote 'parochialism is universal. It deals with the fundamentals.'[1]

> All great civilisations are based on parochialism. To know fully even one field or one land is a lifetime's experience. In the world of poetic experience it is depth that counts, not width. A gap in a hedge, a smooth rock surfacing a narrow lane, a view of woody meadows, the stream at the junction of four small fields – these are as much as a man can fully experience.

Robert Macfarlane, from whose essay this quotation is taken, says that for Kavanagh, 'the parish was not the perimeter, but an aperture: a space through which the world could be seen', though that is not to see sameness in every particular. Patrick McGuinness, in his fragment on Robert Hainaux from his memoir of childhood in Belgium, speaks of someone as typifying 'a certain kind of life and culture ... that mix of industrial and rural that you get in small factory towns' (McGuinness, 2015, p 31) – a cultural mix that rarely figures in social work writing.

Less positively, place also remains for many a site of ambiguity. Recalling how old people move to residential care, McGuinness says: 'My consolation is that my grandmother never knew enough English to feel the painful irony of that foreign word "home" being used to designate the place that would have dislodged her from hers' (McGuinness, 2015, pp 79-80). Speaking about a poem by the local poet, Pirotte – 'probably the first poem I read' – he refers to his own 'malady of time and place'. In response to such maladies, we may retreat

---

[1]   I quote this from a piece in *The Guardian* Review section 30 July 2005, www.theguardian.com/books/2005/jul/30/featuresreviews.guardianreview22.

into small personal spaces. 'I squeezed into that thumb-sized space in the palm of my hand ...' as the poet Ruby Robinson says (Robinson, 2016, from her poem 'Apology') when speaking of her less than happy foster home childhood.

Stepping back to gain a wider angle, we may think of Dannie Abse, the Welsh poet-doctor, whose poem 'Return to Cardiff' (Abse, 1989) 'seemed less a return than a raid on mislaid identities' and:

> where the boy I was not and the man I am not
> Met, hesitated, left double footsteps, then walked on.

Wider still and more bleak, R.S. Thomas laments both place and time ('Welsh Landscapes', Thomas, 1986):

> There is no present in Wales,
> And no future;
> There is only the past,
> Brittle with relics ...
> And an impotent people,
> Sick with inbreeding,
> Worrying the carcase of an old song.

Task Box 6.1: Creative writing on place and space

I have revealed some of my own reading by those we think of as creative writers. Thinking of your own favourites, what illumination does their writing offer to social work in their understanding of place and space?

Globalisation

'Globalisation' is an impoverished term, bowdlerised from its various and tricky meanings. Used daily in the media, it occurs very largely in contexts of economic and financial systems. It is easy to find negative judgements about globalisation in social work. According to Lena Dominelli (2010), it has:

- promulgated a new managerialism;
- disempowered social workers by restricting access to resources;
- increased the techno-bureaucratic nature of practice;
- shifted us away from relational social work;

- turned service users into consumers in a quasi-market;
- reduced solidarity;
- moved away from universal services to residual ones;
- led to an agenda of treating people as responsible for their problems;
- increased the impact on local practice of poverty, the drug trade and trafficking;
- increased the impact of migration.

She scorns the Americanisation of social work, and accuses western academics of talking down local practices. Globalisation, so she laments, turns goods and people into commodities. These trends and others 'bring the global to the local and raise the local to the global arena' (Dominelli, 2010, p 609). The tone is too much like a street demonstration – perhaps what we *do* need on the streets, but not enough. It is too much like a frequent problem in some social work writing – that claims are made but no understanding is offered.

So to what does globalisation refer? While the focus of the media is typically on the financial markets and global trade, a wider scope should include:

- the spread of new forms of non-territorial activity such as the internet, video conferencing, e-commerce, virtual learning;
- the processes whereby geographically distant events and decisions have a growing impact on 'local' life – that is, the growth of social as well as economic and political connectedness;
- the speed or velocity of social activity. High-speed technology is the obvious but not the only manifestation of this. It already is hard for us to appreciate the dramatic shift introduced by electronic communication via email in the 1990s.

Hong and Song (2010) reproduce an argument that globalisation has three contradictions. It leads to:

- social polarisation among and within states, for example through large capital inflows leading to rapid monetary expansion, inflation and widening deficits;
- loss of states' autonomous powers, for example to shield citizens from the negative effects of globalisation. Nation states increasingly react to international forces rather than initiate such forces;
- the decomposition of civil society marked by a growing gap between the base of society and its political leaders and loss of confidence in politicians, seeing them as unable to resolve social problems.

Two important modifications should be noted at this point. First, at the time of writing the growth of political populism in Europe and the US and threats to free trade act as counter-weights to aspects of Hong and Song's argument. Second, globalisation is not only a recent or short-lived phenomenon – though current transformations may be especially far-reaching.[2] Heidegger, for example, accurately prophesied that new communication and information technologies would give birth to novel possibilities for dramatically extending the scope of *virtual reality*. Writing in the late 1960s on the nature of 'a thing', he said:

> Distant sites of the most ancient cultures are shown on film as if they stood this very moment amidst today's street traffic.... The peak of this abolition of every possibility of remoteness is reached by television, which will soon pervade and dominate the whole machinery of communication. (Heidegger, 1971, p 163)

In his analysis, the compression of space increasingly meant that from the perspective of human experience 'everything is equally far and equally near' (p 164). The abolition of distance tended to generate a 'uniform distanceless' in which fundamentally distinct objects became part of a bland homogeneous experiential mass. The loss of any meaningful distinction between nearness and distance contributed to a levelling down of human experience (Heidegger, 1971).

Hence, while 'globalisation' as a term has become commonplace only in the past two or three decades, the idea is not new. Consider the emergence in the 19th and early 20th centuries of high-speed travel (rail and air) or communication (telegraph or telephone). As early as 1839, an English journalist commented on the implications of rail travel by anxiously predicting that as distance was 'annihilated, the surface of our country would, as it were, shrivel in size until it became not much bigger than one immense city' (Schivelbusch, 1977, p 34). A few years later Heinrich Heine, an émigré German-Jewish poet, captured this same experience when he noted:

---

[2] Simon Jeffrey, in an interesting article in *The Guardian* newspaper back in 2002, remarked that 'It was the anti-globalisation movement that really put globalisation on the map. As a word it has existed since the 1960s, but the protests against this allegedly new process, which its opponents condemn as a way of ordering people's lives, brought globalisation out of the financial and academic worlds and into everyday current affairs jargon' (www.theguardian.com/world/2002/oct/31/globalisation.simonjeffery).

[S]pace is killed by the railways. I feel as if the mountains and forests of all countries were advancing on Paris. Even now, I can smell the German linden trees; the North Sea's breakers are rolling against my door. (Cited in Schivelbusch, 1977, p 32)

So what should we think?

Is it possible to achieve justice at a global level? It has become common in this connection to distinguish between *cosmopolitans* and *communitarians*. Cosmopolitans underscore our universal moral obligations to those who reside far away and with whom we share little in the way of language, custom, or culture, arguing that claims to 'justice at home' can and should be applied elsewhere as well. Communitarians by no means deny the need to redress global inequality. Nor do they necessarily deny that the process of globalisation is real. Nonetheless, they doubt that humanity has achieved a rich or sufficiently connected sense of a common fate such that far-reaching attempts to achieve greater global justice (for example, substantial redistribution from the rich to poor, or, to borrow a term that had a short-lived currency at the end of the first decade of this century, 'predistribution') could prove successful.

Dominelli is, on the whole, a communitarian. She welcomes the development, as she sees it, of indigenous practice, but also reminds, helpfully, that 'learning from the experiences of indigenous peoples does not absolve other social workers in the global north from innovating ...' (Dominelli, 2010, p 609). In contrast, Trygged's response is toward cosmopolitanism. He 'argues against an approach that only recognizes context-bound social work.' His main message is 'the importance of developing international social work in the spirit of universalism and critical modernity' (Trygged, 2010, p 645), or as he later expresses it, 'how to be universalist without being imperialist' (p 650), and believes 'it is better to look for what unites people rather than how to preserve diversity' (p 654).

Global standards do not exist in a vacuum; they both reproduce and strive to overcome the inequalities that exist between the industrialized and the developing countries. Yet global standards codify intentions and in the long run may help to unify social work in different parts of the world. (p 652)

A term that came into the language in the late 1980s is the portmanteau word 'glocalisation', similar in some ways to the older expression, 'think globally, act locally', and used to refer to the co-presence of both universalising and particularising tendencies. What might this mean here and now? For agency **senior managers**, this would involve being mindful of how policies are appropriately implemented at the local level, of how local inventiveness needs to go hand in hand with top-down innovation. For **educational leaders**, we need what has been called 'glocal literacy'. For example, **information literacy** means possessing a thorough understanding of the use of the immense variety of tools available for accessing information today, and the ability to think critically about the information they provide. We are perhaps just beginning to see the emergence of some literature in social work that is relevant – Andrew Hill and I have tried to tackle this (Hill and Shaw, 2011). **Political literacy** requires educational and practice leaders who possess familiarity with the various formal and informal processes by which people engage in political issues at different levels of governance as well as an understanding of how to act as empowered participants in the processes that influence, from international down to local decisions and policies. In the broad field of **social welfare**, the question presents itself whether the potential exists to create new social actors and structures that are essentially local in spirit but global in character, capable of responding to local social problems.

Research practices and place

One reason for opening this chapter with a consideration of globalisation is that little work has been attempted regarding how such characteristics shape social work research, outside the research implications of the general arguments about the consequences of the information society for, as Dominelli put it, increasing the techno-bureaucratic nature of practice (compare Parton, 2008a, 2008b). The thoughtful guidelines published by the Association of Internet Researchers ethics committee (Markham and Buchanan, 2012) highlight the contested nature of private/public digital spaces, asking 'Is a blog a public or private space?' Even here, however, there has been a significant revival of recognition of the role of judgement and discretion, through, for example, the interest of Evans and others in Lipsky's earlier notion of street-level bureaucracy (see, for example, Evans, 2011, 2016).

While this is somewhat conjectural, it seems plausible to suggest that international social work practice networks and organisations are held together primarily by shared broad sets of values, while research organisations that cross national borders are brought together by either shared disciplinary and professional interests or by commitments to scholarly rigour. But this may not make for simple transfer of interest and practice between nations. For example, survey models must also be viewed through the prism of western pluralism. It is certainly true that beliefs about society held by English-speaking heirs of a broadly Judeo-Christian civilisation may not be shared by others. Harré (1989, p 23) suggests that members of such societies believe that:

- They are autonomous individuals.
- Despite being trapped in a web of conventions and apparently inexorable natural order, they are agents.
- They have both individually and collectively a past and a future, and so have histories.

The points of common ground with individuals living in Muslim theocracies are difficult to detect.

National characteristics and differences are also pertinent if we take into account the extraordinary extent to which US social work scholars rely on reading work by other US writers to the exclusion of social work scholarship from other countries. Somewhere around 95-98% of citations in US journals by US scholars are of other US scholarship (Shaw, 2014a). Differences occur also when considering what may seem fairly context-free practices. We saw in the previous chapter how Fortune, for example, argues that the task-centred model belongs to the family of evidence-driven and linear intervention models that she regards as being distinctively American rather than the British import of evidence-based practice (Fortune, 2014). There may be some basis for Fortune's assertion. The phrase 'empirical practice', for example, occurs only six times in the *British Journal of Social Work* from 1996 to 2015. The expression 'evidence-based practice', by contrast, occurs 271 times. To touch on a further important research-related consideration, faith-based stances on social work in general and social work science in particular have perhaps been less self-effacing in the US than in most countries in Europe and elsewhere.

More confident understanding of how social work research either varies or is similar from place to place requires greater reflection on what happens when social work research occurs. We tried to contribute to this in the discussion of the nature of research networks and practitioner research in Chapter Four. As Erikson puts it:

> We have to place science in the context of work if we are to understand why it is that scientists will produce knowledge in the way they do. We need to have a grasp of the inward conditions that motivate scientists, the ways in which scientists themselves are making sense of their project, and ... we must have some understanding of the external conditions of science that pattern and structure the vocation of scientists. The interplay of these three factors is what gives science and scientific institutions their character....
> (Erickson, 2002, p 53)

We briefly encountered the conclusions drawn by Edwards and her colleagues regarding the relationship of networks to space in a social work agency in the same chapter. The authors posed the question of how knowledge 'moves around', upstream and downstream, within an organisation: between *levels*, between *strategy and practice*, and between different '*spaces*' or 'fields' within an organisation, for example between child protection teams and teams working with children with a disability (Edwards et al, 2006)? They concluded that:

> Systems for moving knowledge from practice to strategy ... rarely existed. More commonly partnerships relied on individuals to broker knowledge up the system. Consequently knowledge from practice sometimes did not inform strategic work.... Where there were no meetings to enable practitioners to look beyond the boundaries of their own services there was the danger of reliance on old networks, and either a lack of collaboration or misunderstandings when practitioners needed to collaborate. (p 218)

This gives a sense of what they call 'boundary zones' – organisational 'spaces between services where practitioners could meet' (p 193), but of limited space where strategy players and practice players could engage. 'Places where Board members and practitioners met to share ideas were relatively rare' (p 202).

Surveillance

New opportunities for gaining evidence about spatial patterns and behaviours in social work introduce new risks. Foucault, in his explorations of the relationship between knowledge and power spoke of disciplinary power. This is for Foucault a 'technology' aimed at 'how to keep someone under surveillance, how to control his conduct … how to improve his performance … put him where he is most useful' (Foucault, cited in O'Farrell, 2005, p 102). It involves organising space in a particular way with enclosures within which smaller partitions are established (classrooms, wards, cells), and activities organised. Foucault developed the idea of panopticism, where people can be observed but cannot see back – an inspecting gaze exercised through the examination of individualised cases. Social work assessment in residential assessment units can be explored in this way.

Understanding of surveillance is an area where social work ought to draw on scholarship within sociology, in for example the substantial work of David Lyon (see, for example, Lyon, 2001, 2007; Lyon and Bauman, 2013). One of the most sustained social work expositions of this case has been developed by Nigel Parton (see, for example, Parton, 2008a; Parton and Kirk, 2010). With Kirk, he sets out how 'those considered potentially at risk are the subject of increased state surveillance, intervention and control, even though many, if not most of them, are not and will never become 'cases' of the problem' (Parton and Kirk, 2010, p 29). They speak of the 'de-emphasis of the relationship, the abandonment of explanation, and the growth of surveillance' (p 32), such that while the technical requirements in the job have increased, space for professional judgement has decreased and 'social work becomes increasingly involved in ever wide-ranging, complex and unstable systems of surveillance, particularly where such systems are used to enhance strategies for early intervention' (pp 33-4). I quote at greater length:

> With the introduction of ICT there is an expectation that as information becomes more accessible, the agencies, professionals and their decisions should become more transparent and accountable. In the process, there is less discretion for the individual professional for identifying what information is relevant as the required information is predetermined by the structure of the database and the algorithm. The identities of clients as people with needs and problems in contexts are superseded by accounts constructed by the fields that constitute the database…. In the process, the embodied subject is in danger of disappearing and we are left with a variety of surface information which provides little basis for in-depth explanation or understanding. (p 33)

Space and research methods

One of the more interesting trends in research studies of social work has been the prominence afforded to methods that give prominence to the importance of space and place. This can be observed in several ways, including trends in interview methods and applications of ethnography to social work. The strategies of research in social and cultural geography also have enriched some parts of social work research, albeit to rather limited degrees.[3] The growing potential for visual methods has also contributed to exploring places and contexts, using photographs, drawings, maps and videos.

Interviews

The self-interview is one such development. Allet and her colleagues explain the method as follows (Allet et al, 2011). Participants use an audio recorder to 'record themselves responding to a particular topic and to related media, objects and/or spaces' (p 1). They develop a rationale in terms of it providing 'a space away from the usual imperatives of a face-to-face interview' (p 1). Their application of the method was in the context of the association of music and photographs in remembering, so they encouraged participants to move around the house commenting on photos and music as they did so. So as they look at their photographs and listen to music the process 'creates a space in which they can reflect on their memories and cross-temporal associations as they happen, *in situ*' (p 3).

Clark and Emmel refer in helpful detail to **walking interviews**, where the participant gets to show rather than describe the environments that the researcher is interested in, or which make up the spaces that are significant to the participant. Also, placing events, stories and experiences in their spatial context can help participants to articulate their thoughts (Clark and Emmel, 2010, p 2).

Not all developments in research methods point in this direction. Bampton and Cowton neatly capture how the **email interview** 'entails two types of displacement, relating to two fundamental dimensions of human experience. In relation to time, the interactions between interviewer and interviewee are likely to be asynchronous, with pauses of varying lengths between bursts of communication or "episodes"; while in terms of space, the relationship takes place "at a distance"

---

[3]   The examples taken from interviews and ethnography are developed extensively in Shaw and Holland (2014).

through the medium of electronic, screen-based text' (Bampton and Cowton, 2002, para 6). However, they caution that 'Physical remoteness makes the situation very difficult to read' (para 11).

Task Box 6.2: Qualitative methods for social work practice

Check out and read one of the sources by Allet et al (2011) or Clark and Emmel (2010). In conversation with a social work colleague, consider how they might lend themselves to adapting as a form of social work intervention. Link your conclusions with the section on methodological social work practice in Chapter Seven.

Ethnography

Schwab was talking about a different strategy and a school setting, but his remarks transfer well in this connection when he says:

> It is local context that matters – the curriculum will be brought to bear not in some archetypal classroom but in a particular locus in time and space with smells, shadows, seats and conditions outside its walls which may have much to do with what is achieved inside. (Schwab, 1969, p 12)

Take, for example, McMahon's recollections of her research on the unpredictable territory of social work home visits:

> I stood apprehensively in the hallway of a house while two policemen and a worker took an African American child from her parents. I wrote in my notebook, 'Amid the crying, weeping, cursing, and screaming, I stood in the hallway, conscious of my intrusion, not wanting to go in or leave, but uncomfortably aware that I would be seen as a cause of the commotion.' (McMahon, 1998, p 114)

Ethnographies centred around participant observation are often concerned with spatial aspects of social work, such as neighbourhood work and community organising. Qualitative methods are particularly apt within the context of the 'spatial turn' in social sciences in recent decades. Places are understood as relational and complex, with even seemingly quantifiable aspects such as geographic boundaries subject to local and individual dynamic social constructions (Massey, 1991). Geographic Information Systems are increasingly used in social science research. Verd and Porcel (2012), in a study of urban regeneration in Barcelona, added geo-references to qualitative data generated from interviews, urban planning documents, press releases, photographs and memos. This allowed the generation of maps in which quotations and visual images could be located in specific geographical points.

Box 6.1: Spatial understanding of children and risk

In a neighbourhood study of children's safeguarding in Wales, Sally Holland and colleagues explored residents' everyday experiences and perceptions of children's safety and risk, and their interactions with voluntary sector and statutory service providers. Two neighbourhoods were selected that had contrasting socio-demographic features *and* rather different spatial features. For example, the first neighbourhood had open gardens with low walls and shared play spaces. The second had much more individualised play spaces for children. In the following excerpt, the researchers explain how different aspects of the neighbourhood were explored through mobile interviews, interviews of residents in clusters of neighbouring houses, historic documentary data and participant observation of life in the neighbourhoods.

> Particularly *spatial* approaches are embedded in the design. Four examples of how specific qualitative methods can aid our spatial understanding are as follows. Firstly, we have conducted mobile walking and driving interviews with parents, children and community workers. Some of these have included the generation of GPS tracks of the interview routes. Secondly, we have conducted qualitative interviews with residents within micro-localities – clusters of neighbouring houses – about their interactions with their environment and neighbours. This generates data not about 'this *kind of* place' but '*this* place' and starts to build a rich picture of the interactions of perceptions and relationships involved in children's wellbeing at neighbourhood level. Thirdly, we have collected historic data about the places we are researching, through council meeting minutes, newspaper reports and old maps to understand how the intersection of children's welfare and place has evolved and changed over time. Interviews with older residents and activists have also aided this understanding. Fourthly, participant observation by researchers in the community centre, in neighbourhood meetings and walking about neighbourhoods provide

rich descriptions in field notes of neighbourhood life across seasons and at different times of day and evening. (Holland et al, 2011, pp 695-6; emphasis in original)[4]

Social networks have long been of interest to social workers and community organisers. A routine part of many social workers' practice is to draw up 'ecomaps' and 'genograms' with their clients in an attempt to visually represent and understand social contexts (Holland et al, 2011).

Cultural geography

Bingley and Milligan (2007) discuss the advantages of using multi-sensory methodologies in their study into the long-term mental health effects of different kinds of childhood play space. Working with a small group of young people aged 16-21 years old, they used a multi-method approach including practical workshops where the young people took part in a day of woodland activities and artwork sessions. The cross-over with ethnography, and the challenges posed by research with children and young people feed into these developments (see Mandell, 1988 for both these influences).

Geographic perspectives have also developed the fruitful idea of therapeutic landscapes (see, for example, Milligan et al, 2004; Williams, 2007). Social work has taken interest in ecological practice models, but has made too little connection to the ecological research heritage dating from Robert Park's human ecology research at the University of Chicago – so much so that the appearance of Megan Martin's delightful article on 'Crossing the line' strikes the reader almost as a novelty. Martin adopted a writing form that reflects space and movement in the organisation of the text on the page (Martin, 2007).

In an illuminating study of voluntary care, Milligan takes care of the elderly as an example, on the premise that:

> [L]ittle attention has been given to the *inter*-agency relationships between informal and state providers. Still less attention has been given to any detailed examination of how these relationships vary across space and how this impacts on care outcomes for service users. (Milligan, 2001, p 54; emphasis in original)

---

[4]   I reproduce this with the permission of the authors.

She uses the idea of 'dependency networks' as a framework for 'exploring how the inter-relationships between actors operating across space and at differing levels of the care process contribute to local variations in care outcomes' (p 55). This work is grounded in the argument that 'geographical approaches to voluntarism are important for social policy as such approaches argue that *where* events occur matter (for) both their form and outcome' (Milligan and Fyfe, 2004, p 73; emphasis in original).

This underlines the importance of 'socially shared understandings of the normative contours of "proper places" which shape the way people respond to the everyday lived reality of places' (Popay et al, 2003, p 55). The intertwined methodological and substantive dimensions of such commitments are cogently illustrated and exemplified in work on homelessness where people are 'out of place' (Flick and Röhnsch, 2007; Hodgetts et al, 2007).

> Materially and spatially located experiences remind homeless people of who they are, who they want to be, whether they belong and how they are connected or dislocated from others. (Hodgetts et al, 2007, p 711)

Hodgetts and colleagues argue that 'image-based methods are particularly suited where respondents are spatially dispersed and mobile, and where the research requires a narrative that retains a strong sense of personal and social context' (p 712).

Passing mention should also be made of **sounds and silences**. Some attention has been paid to the role of sound in qualitative research (Hall et al, 2008). Sounds are particularly important, they note, in understanding places and these are brought together in the 'soundscape'. Drawing on earlier work by Schafer, Hall and colleagues explain that the soundscape enables researchers and audiences to pay attention to the 'sonic landscape' and 'presents an opportunity to think with sound about concepts of space and the everyday' (2008, p 1030).

There is much potential for social work researchers to use soundscapes with service recipients to understand everyday lived experiences and identities and disrupt normative assumptions about marginalised groups in our societies.[5]

---

[5] While not about social work, it is worth referencing the major UK project on sounds of the seashore, for an example of how rewarding soundscapes can prove (www.nationaltrust.org.uk/features/sounds-of-our-shores).

Reminder from the past

Prone as ever to inflate the significance of the present over the past, we would be wrong to imagine that current awareness of the importance of place and space is a new discovery. To give a single counterweight, Erle Fisk Young (1888-1953) was a graduate student in the University of Chicago sociology department in the second and third decades of the last century, and a lecturer in the Graduate School of Social Service Administration coordinating a course in advanced social case work. He undertook research studies in sociology of which the prominent sociologist Robert Park said 'seem destined to me to change fundamentally our whole conception of case histories' (Park, 1924, p 263). He was at the heart of much of the day-to-day work on drawing up the maps of Chicago that became a central part of the Chicago School's output. Fay Karpf recalled in a 1972 interview (University of Chicago, Department of Sociology) 'Erle Young and I made the first four ecological maps and we really did ourselves proud.... I mean they were beautiful' (compare Young, 1925). Young's report to the funders of his study on Natural Areas and Community Organization shows how he and his mentors such as Ernest Burgess already were thinking in terms that came out in subsequent sociology when he said:

> Practically it raises the question: How far can the present use of arbitrarily chosen units of study (such as census districts, wards, and so on) be replaced in both theoretical and practical investigation by the natural area as a unit? Social service agencies, in particular, will profit by the adoption of such a unit. (University of Chicago, Office of the President. Box 77, Folder 22)[6]

More generally, a comparison of current journals with, for example, a scan of the early books and journals in anthropology (for example, Malinowski) and sociology (for example, W.I. Thomas) shows how little the methodological interest in visual methods has percolated through to research practice, compared with the almost routine use of visual images in early articles.

---

[6] For a recognition of Young's contribution as part of a sociological social work period in the US, see Shaw (2015b).

Making practical sense

Perhaps the most readily mined set of inferences from this chapter is found in the final section. An almost chronic limitation of social work interviews is the degree to which they reply on what is said. Walking interviews and the self-interview both suggest ways of adding considerable depth and meaning to the standard practice interview format. Photographic methods and some applications of mapping also have a practice role. To develop the extent and value of such applications would need reading the full text of the relatively brief sources cited in the chapter.

To convey an adequate sense of the issue at stake here, I need to draw on a distinction, the practice implications of which I have developed fairly extensively elsewhere, and which forms part of the next chapter. This is between applying the *findings* of research – the usual way in which we think of research applications – and 'applying' the *methods* of research. 'Applying' is in inverted commas because I do not have in mind a one-for-one carry-over of how one does research to how one does social work, but a form of practice that requires a clear but sometimes imaginative and creative 'translation'. I will hold the argument at this stage and return to it in Chapter Seven.

The other general challenge that I believe is raised by the material covered earlier in this chapter is the extent to which it fills out as extensively as anywhere else in the book a principle that I introduced in the Introduction – that is, the value of thinking across boundaries whether they be between the social sciences or in work that invites engagement between social work and what we think of as creative writing.

SEVEN

Sociological social work: a case example

This penultimate chapter will take up a theme that follows from Chapters Five and Six. Whereas there we think of social work in relation to time and place, this chapter will consider social work in relation to other fields and disciplines. The underlying assumption – that I will set out in straightforward ways – is that social work research and practice have much to gain by welcoming their relationship to other bordering fields. The example I will give is sociology. I will deal with the issues in three ways.

First, I will outline the scope and nature of what sociological social work might encompass.

Second, I will look at how sociologists and social workers have understood their relationship. To ensure readers can gain from this material, the heart of this section will be an introduction to a series of sociologists who, in my view, are doing work that treats social work as of sociological interest.

Third, I will outline a case I have developed in detail elsewhere regarding ways in which the **methods of inquiry** that are associated with qualitative sociological research are open to 'translation' such that they may become a form of practice.

In an important way, this chapter stands apart from other chapters in this book. The broad aim of the book is to make accessible ideas and debates that in most respects have taken place between some social work scholars and members of related communities and disciplines. The book reaches for distinctiveness based on the level of writing and audience rather than by bringing in completely new ideas and arguments. This chapter continues in this vein, but offers a position that has had very little attention in the social work literature and has not impinged on social work practice beyond the margins. I will pursue an argument for sociological social work, while recognising the relative strangeness of the term.

The chapter follows closely the outline in the abstract. After outlining the scope and nature of what sociological social work might encompass, we turn attention to how sociologists and social workers have understood their relationship. The chapter closes with examples of ways in which the methods of inquiry that are associated with qualitative sociological research are open to 'translation' such that they may become a form of practice. To express the basic distinction at issue in a grossly simple way, most work on sociology and social work, from a social work standpoint, has its terminus on how sociology may shape what social workers know and believe. Sociological social work terminates on what social workers might *do* as a sociological practice.

Given the scale of the topic, the very preliminary nature of work in the field, and the restriction of a few thousand words, this chapter is rather like what I have elsewhere called a 'cartoon' (Shaw, 2014c), taking 'cartoon' in the early sense of a preparatory drawing for a piece of art – of a study or model that in the carrying to the next stage will enable the craftsperson or artist to accurately link the component parts of the composition – hoping, I may add, that I 'don't end up a cartoon in a cartoon graveyard.'[1]

Points of the compass for sociological social work

There are several stories that could be told – about gender relations between sociology and social work; about scholarly relationships; about social reform and the respective roles of social work and sociology; or about the very place of social work and social science within the university. But our attention in this chapter is on what in some ways is a more difficult question regarding forms of practice and intervention. I do not, for a moment, want to claim that sociology and social work are part of one and the same enterprise. Albion Small, the first head of the sociology department at the University of Chicago, was correct, at least in principle, when he remarked on the existence of 'practical social workers who have but a vague notion of society in general, and who consequently cannot properly be called sociologists' (Small, 1903, p 472). Nor do I believe we should even aspire to a circumstance in which sociology and social work coexist in perfect amity. Neither should we wish to draw a line from 80 or 90 years ago and teleport various figures to the present. Burrow carefully remarks that 'We may properly ask why we are not like our ancestors; there seems something

[1] A line from Paul Simon's song 'You Can Call Me Al' (Graceland album), www.paulsimon.com/track/you-can-call-me-al-6/.

odder about asking why our ancestors were not like us' (Burrow, 1970, p xxii). 'A search for friends in the past' (Burrow, 1970, p 19) is legitimate and interesting but it easily slides into an exploitative use of history and leads to a tone that 'is often harsh with the grinding of axes' (p 43).

But the 'So what?' question is not without answer. There are several ways in which encounters may and ought to take place between social work and sociology. These include:

- straining to enact a certain kind of interdisciplinary relationship, a theme we pick up at a more general level in the final chapter;
- developing methodological social work practice;
- hearing occasional sociological frontier conversations;
- shared theorising.

Expressed generally, my aspiration is for a kind of practice in which sociological theory comes together with social work aims, and how social work practitioners – and we might add teachers – can and should engage in a sociologically thinking way, and bring a sociological sensibility and orientation to their world. Thus how do sociological frameworks enrich our understanding of social work as a general help system? A valuable example of such thinking is Schirmer and Michailakis' article on the social work help system in which the authors outline and apply the thinking of Niklas Luhmann (Schirmer and Michailakis, 2015a, 2015b), which elsewhere they apply to questions of loneliness (Schirmer and Michailakis, 2016). A sociological sensibility will operate at different levels such as time, the environment, community and identity. Dunk-West and Verity (2013) introduce issues at this level through their treatment of themes of critical theory, social change and globalisation. In their central chapters, they address identity, organisational contexts, values, community and capitalism. But if it is to take us beyond middle-range stances, how might a sociological sensibility make social work practice different? Dunk-West and Verity's work strikes out in interesting directions, but it lacks grounding and hence we do not hear the voices of those on either the receiving or giving ends of social work. Neither does it say much about what one should *do* with it all. Sociological social work will need to open up how it might drive day-to-day practice–theory interchange, the ways in which the social work case is practically 'organised', and how such social work takes place with problems that tend to be seen primarily in individual terms.

Frontier conversations

Social work, throughout its time, has been tempted by what Ernest Burgess (the Chicago sociologist) long ago described as an 'atomic view of the individual' (Burgess, 1928, p 525). Sociology and social work began 'not as distinct fields but as part of a general impulse for social science that emerged out of the reform activism of the nineteenth century. What we today take for granted as the "natural" division of social science into separate disciplines, including sociology and social work, was a decades-long development out of that original impulse' (Lengermann and Niebrugge, 2007, p 63). What counts as 'social work' or 'sociology' 'does not await in limbo the order that will free it ... it does not preexist itself, held back by some obstacle at the first edges of light' (Packer, 2011, p 347).

We saw in Chapter Five that our present ways of thinking about the apparently 'natural' boundaries between social work and sociology are, in fact, not 'natural' at all. But there continues to be a tendency to see the divergence of sociology and social welfare 'as simply an example of the division of labour concomitant with social progress' (Burrow, 1970, p 102).

> The history of the social sciences is still left largely a prey to the Whig interpretation of history.... The impression conveyed is that the history of the social sciences is to be written by isolating 'anticipations' of modern concepts and methods from the irrelevant, because outmoded, theories of which they formed a part. (Burrow, 1970, p 19)

These ways of thinking about the fields within which we find our identity has led often to a mutual distancing. Edith Abbott, the early dean of the School of Social Service Administration in Chicago, is interesting, not because she was unusual (although in some ways she certainly was), but because she was unequivocal in her remarks. Indeed, like not a few of her successors down the decades, she was on occasion prone to assert a rather dismissive stance towards sociology. On one occasion, when speaking to her fellow social work deans, she lamented that:

> Some of those whom I am tempted to call our 'near' social science friends — because of course I do not consider such persons scientific — insist that social research in the field of social treatment must be carried on *for* and not *by* social

workers whose professional field is under discussion. They even say that their untrained students are more competent to use the records of social agencies, to say what these records do or do not mean, than are the social workers themselves ... I do not say that every social worker is a gifted researcher. Alas, no – but of how many of our social science colleagues can this be said? (Abbott, 1931, p 170-1; emphasis in original)

Corresponding remarks can be found on the part of sociologists. Robert Faris, writing a history of early sociology in Chicago, was speaking of the 'transition from a pre-scientific to a scientific stage in sociology' when he referred to how the early humanitarian 'pull' in sociology had led to 'the not uncommon linking into one university department of sociology and professional training for social work'. He dismissed the 'hopelessly emotional' character of much early work, referring to the 'grand survey movement' in which sociologists 'left most of the activity to welfare workers, administrators and others' (Faris, 1967, p 7). Interviewed around 1972, the sociologist Walter Reckless recalled something of this sociological arrogance, at least among graduate students.

> ... the sociology students all felt this was crazy stuff, do you see what I mean? It had no university standing. This you could understand; this was one of the earliest schools of social work ... in the country, and the opinion among the sociology students was that social work was just sort of a fantasy and was not a university subject. Unfortunately, don't you see? (University of Chicago, Department of Sociology)

In 'the ascendant reconstruction of sociology's past' (Lengermann and Niebrugge, 2007, p 67), sociology and social work are seen as each developing in stages with their own internal logic, whether with intellectual and theoretical concern to understand society, or from practical concern with effectively administering aid. Suspicion of 'do-gooders' was to persist. Crompton recalls that in its early years, the British Sociological Association 'included many non-sociologists as members, who at the time I heard described (somewhat disparagingly) as "do-gooders, vicars and social workers"' (Crompton, 2008, p 1218) – which was 'perhaps paradoxical' given that 'the aim in establishing the journal [that is *Sociology*] was precisely to distance itself from this "public"' (Crompton, 2008, p 1225).

In a series of interesting interviews with British figures who were around in the early decades of the 20th century, we hear Eileen Younghusband, speaking of the London School of Economics (LSE), saying:

> They were marvellous teachers of course, in those days. Hobhouse, Ginsburg, Laski, Malinowski, Westermarck, Eileen Power, Tom Marshall, Bernard Hart, and so on. So it was immensely stimulating … absolute galaxy of talent. (WiseARCHIVE. The Cohen Interviews)

She adds a significant caveat, saying:

> [There was] absolutely nothing that linked all that to the kind of level at which social workers would be working. Of course, there were the social surveys of the period, but there really was nothing applicable in the day to day practice of social workers. (WiseARCHIVE. The Cohen Interviews)

But the evidence – spasmodic and incomplete as it is – suggests there were multiple 'social works' just as there was more than one sociology. Clement Brown, in the same series of interviews, is here speaking of her experience teaching on the LSE mental health course following a stay in the US:

> From time to time I was aware of criticism of my own emphasis as being too much concerned with the relationship between social circumstances and individual problems, this being sometimes described as 'too sociological' in outlook. (WiseARCHIVE. The Cohen Interviews)

Her remark on this is 'I suppose the issue turned a good deal on the extent to which Freudian psycho-analysis should be regarded as one of the most important approaches to the understanding of human behaviour', and she concludes in ways that sustain a structural account:

> Looking back on a life's professional experience of social work, I think what impresses me is the kind of dilemma that there is always between concentration on the very subtle difficult business of understanding individual variation

and individual ways of meeting the needs of individuals, with the very obvious knowledge that social conditions are constantly creating the kind of difficulties with which we are dealing. (WiseARCHIVE. The Cohen Interviews)

This hardening of boundaries and cross-border positions was most explicitly and influentially represented in later years by C. Wright Mills' famous critique of social pathologists that we outlined in Chapter Three. His article can fairly be treated as transcending transatlantic divides,[2] and illustrating how sociologists who may never have read social work texts took up a position as given – that social work in its entirety was no longer, even if it had once been, relevant to sociology – a position that was to appear in bowdlerised form in the remarks Crompton heard some years later. Mills believed that the work of Mary Richmond afforded 'a clue as to why pathologists tend to slip past structure to focus on isolated situations, why there is a tendency for problems to be considered as problems of individuals, and why sequences of situations were not seen as linked into structures' (Mills, 1943, p 170), in that by emphasising 'the whole' this assumes there are many parts. This leads to a multi-causal approach, which in turn implies that social change will need multiple considerations and will not be easy.

Sociological social workers

Should this last couple of pages be seen as darkly pessimistic, there are those in both sociology and social work, past and present, who have taken a mutually more interested approach. Chambon suggests that we ought to approach this work by recognising how 'The activities at the borders of a field are concrete manifestations of movements in knowledge in the academic sense ... and express ways in which members of the field relate to broader social relations (responsiveness and agency in the societal order of relations' (Chambon, 2012, p 1). However, borders are not simply established in relation to external disciplines:

The boundaries and borrowings from outside disciplines and practices reflect movements from within the field – the constant repositioning of agents and spheres of influence, and of values being pursued – such that there is a parallel

---

[2]   It was standard reading on my Sheffield undergraduate programme in the 1960s.

between the outside boundaries and the partitions that exist inside the field: borders without and borders within. Both types of borders discriminate between types of knowledge, horizons, disciplinary subcultures, and the accompanying sets of differentiated practices. (Chambon, 2012, p 1)

It may help if we run through several of the individuals – often too little known – who, both past and present, act as exemplars of the approach I believe usefully places social work in a wider disciplinary field. In saying 'too little known', I intentionally avoid familiar names from the US such as Jane Addams and Mary Richmond, not because their significance has been fully understood (compare Branco, 2016) but to show that the net should be cast wider than conventionally assumed.

From the past

I want to very briefly introduce Harriett Bartlett, Stuart Queen, Ada Sheffield, Erle Fisk Young and Pauline Young. All from the US, I realise. We have met some of these already, especially Ada Sheffield (Chapter Five). Readers may think of others to add. Alice Salomon holds a central place in the development of social work in Germany and with an influence and reputation that extends beyond that country's variously drawn boundaries over the past century. Yet important as she is, her sociological sensibilities seemed restricted.

[Alice Salomon] took the lead in establishing the German Academy for Social and Pedagogical Work for Women, which quickly acquired a division for research. Under her guidance it published numerous studies of family life and the disruptive influences to which it was being subjected, for which much of the inspiration emanated from the works of Edith Abbott and Sophonisba Breckinridge of the School for Social Service Administration at the University of Chicago. (Lee, 2004, p 6)[3]

Prior to her emigration to the US in 1937, she had designed her curriculum 'with a view to fostering practical knowledge of and feasible solutions to social problems, insisting on the need for a foundation

---

[3] Her version of feminism drew on ideas regarding the complementarity of the roles of women and men, and this set her apart from the egalitarian forms of feminism that were more prominent in the US in the middle decades of the last century.

of objective knowledge that would not depend on partisanship for its acceptability' (Lee, 2004, p 3).

Ada Sheffield (1869-1943) was Boston-based.[4] She worked in the Boston charities field and was director of a new Mother's Aid Program. Her tenure was short-lived when in 1914 the city's first Catholic mayor did not reappoint her. She was director of the Research Bureau on Social Case Work. She authored two significant books in that period – *The social case history: Its construction and content* (1920) and *Case study possibilities: A forecast* (1922). The latter is a brief but remarkable text that drew appreciative comments from Ernest Burgess. She later (1937) wrote *Social insight in case situations.* She was the eldest sister of the poet T.S. Eliot – Ada Eliot Sheffield was her full name. Her brother regarded her as 'a very exceptional woman'.

Erle Fisk Young, 1888-1953, was a graduate student in the University of Chicago sociology department in the second and third decades of the last century, and a lecturer in the Graduate School of Social Service Administration, coordinating a course in advanced social case work. He undertook research studies in the sociology department of which, as we noticed earlier, Robert Park said 'seem destined to me to change fundamentally our whole conception of case histories' (Park, 1924, p 263). He moved to the University of Southern California where he appears to have spent the whole of his life thereafter. He wrote almost entirely in the field of social work, including several editions of *The social workers' dictionary*, on family case work, race, and more broadly on social welfare. He was married to Pauline Young, with whom he completed some co-authoring.

Stuart Queen, 1890-1987, was born in Fredonia, Kansas. He entered Pomona College in 1906, majoring in Greek. In 1908, Queen transferred to the University of Nebraska at Lincoln, where he developed his lifelong interest in sociology. Queen received a PhD in sociology from the University of Chicago in 1919. Queen was Professor of Social Economy and director of the School of Social Work at Simmons College (1920-22), Professor of Sociology at University of Kansas (1922-1930), and Professor of Sociology at Washington University, St Louis (1932-58). Queen's published works include an early book on the county jails and *Social work in the light of history* (1922), and a number of papers on social work's relation to sociology. His unpublished – and apparently unread – autobiography is in the Special Collections at the University of Chicago.

---

[4]   I have written about these people in varying detail elsewhere. Here I simply sketch the outlines of their lives and work.

Pauline Young (née Vislick), 1896-1977, was born in Russian Poland (what we now call Belarus). I know nothing of her early life, but she migrated to US in 1913, and married in 1918. She had three children. She entered the University of Chicago for her degree in 1915 and credits the influence of Small, Park and W.I. Thomas. She worked as a family case worker in 1917 through to 1918 and graduated in 1919. She worked as a researcher between 1918 and 1925 in both Chicago and Los Angeles, where she gained her MA in 1925. In 1928, she wrote an article asking whether case records should be written in the first person in the same year that Burgess was writing on that theme (Burgess, 1928). She dedicated her book on interviewing (1935) to him – as 'teacher and friend.'

Harriett Bartlett, 1897-1987, was a moving force in the fields of medical social work and social work education. Born in Lowell, Massachusetts, she graduated from Vassar in 1918. In 1920, she earned a Social Service Certificate from the London School of Economics and Political Science. She was awarded an MA in sociology from the University of Chicago in 1927 and in 1969 received an honorary doctorate from Boston University. From 1947 to 1957, Bartlett was a professor and director of Medical Social Work at Simmons College School of Social Work in Boston. Her major study on social work practice, conducted during the 1960s, resulted in the publication of perhaps her best-known book, *The common base of social work practice*.

Part of the reason for introducing these people is to invite the reflection that, on discovering that our family is larger than and somewhat different from what we knew, what if anything ought we to do about it? I am not sure how far these individuals saw their standpoints as presenting a consciously taken alternative position to what was developing around them. Nor do I think they were particularly aware that they occupied common ground with one another. Finally, they did little to sustain or develop their positions, and, by the time the US entered the Second World War, little was left to be seen.

These scholars held coherent, though not identical, frames of reference – 'coherent' in the sense that Foucault speaks of a discourse, as groups of verbal performances that are not linked to one another grammatically (as sentences) or at a logical level (as formally coherent) or even psychologically (for example, as a conscious project) but at the statement level, as a way of speaking (Foucault, 2002). In various respects, their work can be seen as giving a sociological 'shape' to social work practice. This is so in three central ways:

- through their understanding of social environments;
- in the meaning they gave to the 'case';
- in the direct practice of social work intervention.

We will expand the third point later. On the environment, Ada Sheffield foreshadowed later standpoints regarding social work as focusing on the person in the environment. She places centre-stage 'personality and situation' – 'the individual's biographical endowment, and the relationships which show the interplay between this native endowment and his social milieu'. 'Case workers should think of the relation between individual and milieu and when dictating to their stenographer bear these relations in mind.' This 'holds promise … of a gain in power to give practical help to clients….' (Sheffield, 1922, p 14).

In a letter of February 1928 to the sociologist L.L. Bernard, Pauline Young concluded as follows:

> While in the field as social worker, social investigator, or research worker I was strongly impressed with the complexity of the social forces underlying social situations, with the necessity for studying these situations objectively[5] rather than evaluatively, and in their entire social setting rather than as isolated problems....

Bartlett recalled: 'We were social workers who came out of case work but … through our interest had an urge … to see things more broadly, to see people not just [as] personalities but people who were working and living and growing up in a social environment'. Bartlett had worked for some years as a social worker in London and Massachusetts before taking her sociology masters at Chicago in 1926-27. Asked in 1972 why she opted to take that path rather than register in the Graduate School of Social Service Administration, she said:

> I preferred to go into the social science approach rather than the school of social work, which was very early then. They were pretty well involved with social welfare programs and things like that, and not themselves working out the concepts and principles as much as I wanted. It was more directly service and operational. (University of Chicago, Department of Sociology)

---

[5] By 'objectively', Young, like most of her contemporaries, meant something broader than later meanings, using it more or less as equivalent to 'scientifically'.

Sociologists were 'seeking to come closer to real social experience.... It was good for me to try to understand without trying immediately to change or influence the situation' (University of Chicago, Department of Sociology).

Stuart Queen protested that 'Perhaps the most important reason why social work has not yet become a profession is the persistence of the apprenticeship system' which produces social workers 'ignorant of the relation of social work in general to the community life as a whole' (Queen, 1922, p 25).

Sheffield, from 'the influence of schools of social work and of sociologists' (Sheffield, 1922, p 38), argued that 'case-work agencies ... will gradually become what may be described as social laboratories' where 'study of ... cases would go on simultaneously with treatment'. She realised that when sociologists use words like 'personality', they are not thinking of free agents but 'established modes of activity – within which personality and circumstance are inseparable terms'. Personality is 'a web-like creation of self, interacting with other selves in a succession of situations' (p 10). As with almost all the key figures of the time, Harriet Bartlett valued the sociological stance on the idea of the case:

> I'm glad I came at the time that the case study was regarded as a professional and possibly scientific instrument. There were ways of evaluating this material; it could be other than just used for helping people, trying to understand. (University of Chicago, Department of Sociology)

To the present

It is relatively familiar to think of social work in relation to social constructionism (see, for example, Parton and O'Byrne, 2000; Witkin, 2017). But none of the contemporary advocates of this position may recognise the interrupted line back to those such as Sheffield and Pauline Young. Young remarked that 'facts are facts only in a world of discourse' (Young, 1928/1929, p 499). Sheffield anticipated a constructionist stance when she said of the case worker that 'selection of facts amounts to an implicit interpretation of them' (Sheffield, 1922, p 48), and quotes herself as saying that:

> [t]he traditions and training of the observer more or less condition the *nature* of the fact-items that make their appearance.... In this sense the subject-matter of much

social study is unstable. Not only do two students perceive different facts, they actually in a measure make different facts to be perceived.

The exploration of the idea of the social situation finds later resonance in some of social work's application of systems theory (for example, Siporin, 1972, 1975) and in ecological social work. Murdach draws out an element from the 1890s onwards when there was concern to 'develop both a "scientific" as well as a "social" approach to social work direct practice' (Murdach, 2007, p 211). He discusses Jane Addams, Mary Richmond, Ada Sheffield, Eduard Lindeman and Mary Parker Follett – 'working together or under each other's influence, they pioneered efforts to forge a new "situational" approach to social work practice' (p 211). Murdach recognises Sheffield as 'the major spokesperson for the situational, or as it was called, the "sociological" approach to social work practice' (p 213), and makes the interesting corrective that it was the:

> inclusion of community outreach and development as a necessary and complementary part of all direct practice that set the situational view of social work apart from current, more psychologically oriented approaches and also from the more abstract versions of systems as well as ecological, empowerment, quasi-Marxist, and social constructionist theory popular in social work today. (p 216)

Max Siporin made recurring connections to the significance of Sheffield's contribution. He takes up her concept of the 'total situation' understood as an overall dynamic field of experience 'of interacting people and circumstances' (Siporin, 1975, p 151). He directly follows her position on situation analysis in his elaboration of ecological systems theory (for example, Siporin, 1972).

The debts are not always direct. Noel Timms' work has received fresh recognition in the present decade.[6] Timms spent a short period working in mental health social work before moving into the university world in the UK. He wrote prolifically, producing books that broke fresh ground. His important *oeuvre* is not typical of social work scholarship. In unexpected ways, he constantly set the terms of reference for what on the face of it were standard social work texts. My early research

---

[6] His 1967 text was reprinted by Routledge in 2014. A special issue of the journal *Qualitative Social Work* focused on his work in 2014.

and writing was influenced in several ways by the angles of vision, the 'gaze', that he brought to thinking about and doing social work practice and research. He immediately seems distant from much of social work and from standard social science and social work portrayals of the relationship between the two. His inaugural lecture in 1972 on his move from the London School of Economics to Bradford University expressed this clearly. He confesses his personal 'delineation of social work as concerned with understanding rather than information, and understanding not necessarily with a "practical" or predetermined end in view' (Timms, 1972, pp 1-2). He complains that social work is 'a field of study characterized by conceptual affluence and propositional poverty' and puts forward a notion of social work not unlike some earlier ways of understanding sociology. We noted earlier in this book his remark that 'We should consider social work as primarily neither an applied science nor simple good works but a kind of practical philosophising' (p 3). He also claims a position that if implemented would have been far-reaching – that 'Social work education not only failed itself, it could also have been the active and sustaining source from which the study of sociology ... developed within British universities' (p 3). But taking this position, he believes, is not to hand the social worker over to the 'rather indifferent imperialism of the sociologist' (p 4). His early book on a sociological approach to social problems (Timms, 2014 [1967]) has been cited but a handful of times. This is in part a product of the distorted weighting given by today's too-easy access to virtual 'findability'.[7]

Rather different are those who write about social work without wearing their sociological agenda on their sleeves. A very good example can be found in the career work of Nigel Parton. He has set this out in various places. His development of the idea of constructive social work practice – set out as a practice text in Parton and O'Byrne (2000) – has been set in its context in his 2007 chapter (Parton, 2007). He looks back over his career concern with child protection in a 2014 article (Parton, 2014).

Task Box 7.1: Your debts

Bring to mind the social work writing that has most shaped your own thinking and practice. What debts to other disciplines can you detect in that writing?

---

[7]   I have discussed this book in Shaw (2014b).

Sociologists of and for social work

Why might it be that sociology has demonstrated a sustained interest in sociology when related to medicine, but little to social work? The answer is not obvious. One might think that medicine has status and power, and sociology gains intellectual momentum by attaching itself to medicine's coat-tails. Doubtless so, but this fails to explain fully. For example, there has been much work on the sociology of education – like social work, a field once generally labelled a semi-profession – whereas there has been much less, by comparison, on the sociology of a prestigious profession such as law.[8] There has been a trickle of texts by sociologists that examine social work; however, 'what is missing is a sociological scholarship which adopts social work theory, practice, or methods' (de Montigny, forthcoming).

Task Box 7.2: Sociologists' interest in social work

How much interest have sociologists in your country shown in social work? Assuming that by and large this will be rather limited, why do you think that is the case, bearing in mind the remarks in the previous paragraph?

In the following paragraphs, I will briefly introduce one or two sociologists from the past who regarded social work as of interest, not simply because their field might be thought to offer something of value to social work – a kind of intellectual service industry underwritten by the curriculum requirements of professional programmes – but because of a mutuality of interest obtained. I will then offer a corresponding sketch of sociologists writing today of whom something similar might be said. In Chapter Five, we encountered Stuart Chapin, who, perhaps unwittingly, developed the case for a form of experimental sociology that has continued cogency for social work. Ernest Burgess, the Chicago sociologist active over five decades of the past century, also has figured from time to time in this book.[9]

Frederick Thrasher, another Chicago figure, bears reference in this connection. He was known best for his doctoral work that resulted

---

[8]   The Wikipedia essay on the sociology of law illustrates how the field shifts between various identities (https://en.wikipedia.org/wiki/Sociology_of_law).
[9]   Burgess is an important figure, whose engagement with social work has been grossly under-recognised (compare Shaw, 2009).

in *The gang* (Thrasher, 1927). While he generally took a position that insisted on a conventional distinction between sociology and social work (for example, Thrasher, 1928a), I think it is possible to make three general claims about Thrasher's work, which yields, like Chapin's work, a contribution that may not have been part of a conscious agenda on his part. First, it paints a picture of a community of civic and scholarly enterprise marked by mutual reciprocity and a sense of shared endeavour even if not agreed standpoints. Second, *The gang* affords a record of urban research practice. In both these respects, I concur with Dimitriadis (2006, p 335) when he concludes that Thrasher 'returns us to questions of radical context, the multiple webs of influence and association that so marked studies of the period'. Finally, sociological research at Chicago in the 1920s included a welfare and interventionist mission. On the final point, one of the most significant characteristics of much American sociology in that period is the way it constantly wrestles with its responsibility for presenting a constructive program for social advance through what the sociologist Ernest Burgess and others spoke of as 'practical sociology'. Thrasher describes his study as a 'survey' (1927, p 487) – a term that carried special significance very different from how sample surveys are understood today. Ernest Burgess set out an early plea for social surveys in which he sought to 'call attention to the possibilities within the social survey for service by departments of sociology' and outlined 'a general plan of organization by which the sociologist may best co-operate with the community' (Burgess, 1916, p 492). While Thrasher does not follow the pattern advocated by Burgess, he devotes considerable space to arguments for 'Attacking the problem' (chapter XXII) and 'Crime prevention' (chapter XXIII). Intervention, he insists, needs a 'high degree of intelligence and understanding' (Thrasher, 1927, pp 490-1). He takes what we would now call a community systems approach on the grounds that it is 'impossible to control one factor without dealing with all the others' (p 491). His starting point is that the gang's 'existence must be recognized and some sort of place must be made for it in the life of the community' (p 496). He speaks of the person as 'an individual with status' (p 499), but goes a step further and says that it is not only necessary to study the delinquent as a person, merely to understand him; it is also essential to deal with him as a person in any practical situation demanding the formulation of a program of treatment. 'He must not be treated as if he existed in a social vacuum ...' (p 499).[10]

[10] Thrasher gives a lifelike and amusing account of how he established rapport with gang members (Thrasher, 1928b). The nearest orientation to such practice today may be that found in the work of Howard Williamson (Williamson, 2004). I have explored Thrasher's contribution at some length in Shaw (2011).

A rather different but useful contribution was made by the sociologist Robert MacIver. MacIver at Columbia University found the borders of the fields intrinsically interesting and challenging. He started from the position that 'The relation of sociology to social work is that of a science to an art' (MacIver, 1931, p 1). Extracting phrases from his book, the comparison is set out in Figure 7.1.

Figure 7.1: MacIver on sociology and social work

Social work as art	Sociology as science
'manipulates, controls and changes'	'seeks only to understand'
'individualizes'	'generalizes'
'lives in its concrete embodiments whether it be sculptured stone or the changed conduct of human beings'	'lives in abstract relationships which it discovers irradiating the concrete world'

I set this out not to recommend, but to understand premises in MacIver's thinking.[11] He seems to think of 'art' in ways that are focused on an agenda of change. Science 'can never answer the essential preliminary question, should this objective itself be sought?' (MacIver, 1931, p 3). 'Science is no ready reckoner. It never offers immediate solutions to the problems of living. It never responds to our last-minute appeals' (p 13). Yet social science for the social worker 'helps us to clear our eyes, to see things steadily and whole, to interpret situations *as though* we lacked the emotions which make us want to interpret them' (p 4). Sociology enables the social worker to 'advocate further goals while still doing the day's work' and gives 'a background of intellectual convictions' (p 7). He sees two ways in which the sociologist may cooperate with the social worker:

- by gaining 'an orientation to his task, a greater comprehension ... a broader knowledge ... and this some safeguard against illusive hopes and immature enthusiasms' (p 10); and
- by obtaining 'specific aid from the studies made in the field of his own interest' (p 11).

While this may seem too restrictive, he does emphasise various 'ways in which social work can cooperate with sociology in the extension of our knowledge of society' (MacIver, 1931, p 81).

---

[11] Timms' discussion of social work as science or art (Timms, 1968) remains one of the most stimulating entry points on this question.

- '[T]he social worker can help to classify the types of social situation' (p 81). It is the social worker's 'direct contact with many concrete situations' that helps on this. This is not mere taxonomy but 'demands high powers of observation and ... an appropriate descriptive vocabulary' (p 87).
- S/he 'can help us to study the processes of group life' (p 82). Again, 'sociologists ... lack the opportunity to do so which the social worker possesses. Large-scale investigations do not bring us close to it. Statistical information cannot yield this knowledge.... It is only those who are in a position to use the case method ... who can open out for us its possibilities' (pp 82-3).
- 'The social worker can throw light on social causation.' In social work, 'Every step on the road is an experiment' (p 83). Social causation requires the social worker to have interest in the underlying conditions and causes. MacIver rates this the most highly of the three, and says 'it should determine his whole approach' (p 93).

There are occasional examples of interest from European scholars. Paul Halmos is among the more consequential of these. A Hungarian-born sociologist who spent most of his career in British universities, he wrote extensively on solitude and privacy, the sociology of science (and of sociology), the mass media, professionalism and social change, and the penal services. Perhaps his best-known books are *The faith of the counsellors* (Halmos, 1965) and *The personal service society* (Halmos, 1970). Both books develop his concern with the growing function of counselling as a sociological category. Once staple reading on social work programmes in the UK, Halmos has disappeared from view, probably because he was regarded as unduly conservative, but his work is ripe for a comprehensive review.

The final backwards look is towards settlement sociology. Lengermann and Niebrugge (2002, 2007) place 'settlement sociology' at the heart of a critical history narrative of the relationship of sociology and social work in the US. The elements of this history are that:

- The settlements provided a location for both social work and sociology.
- Settlements sought to reform society using knowledge from social science. This produced a 'science of reform'.
- While settlements were part of emerging sociology and social work, they were marginalised from both by their activist stance.
- This all 'turned on a particular politics of gender' (Lengermann and Niebrugge, 2007, p 94).

Within this, Jane Addams and the Hull-House Settlement are placed as the major actors. The American settlements – 413 by 1910 – were mainly a women's field in terms of residents, volunteers and head residents. This shaped both their kind of sociology and their interpretation of social work. This narrative sees settlement sociology 'as complete a school as any in the history of the discipline' (Lengermann and Niebrugge, 2007, p 98). 'Settlement social scientists conceived of their project as a seamless combination of theory and practice in the service of social reform' (p 107).

On the demise of this 'school', Lengermann and Niebrugge say, 'It is an irony of history that eventually they would be relegated to the margins of sociology because they were "too practical" or "applied", and to the margins of social work because they were "too theoretical" or "abstract"' (p 107), such that 'What finally explains their erasure from the history of sociology is partly a politics of gender, partly a politics of knowledge, and partly a politics of professionalization' (p 110).

21st-century sociology on social work

Talking of contemporary figures risks either offending – or even causing a sigh of relief from – those not mentioned. For purely illustrative purposes, I want to mention Andrew Abbott, Stephen Turner, Daniel Cefai, Jay Gubrium and Michael Bloor – each for different reasons.

Andrew Abbott

The example I want to take is his piece on the idea of boundaries in understanding the emergence and nature of social work. Speaking of the US, Andrew Abbott lists some who were at the 1884 meeting of the National Conference of Charities and Corrections – 'everything conceivably related to social reform ... is contained in this meeting somewhere' (Abbott, 1995, p 546). But by 1912, 'we find a major change'. 'Many aspects of welfare-related work present in the earlier lists are going or gone' while other new links appear, such as psychiatry. 'This set of connections is the great problem of social work history. Why was it that certain task areas became part of social work and other parts did not?' (p 546).

Abbott is atypical as a sociologist who early in his career 'began to find social work knowledge and psychological knowledge ... interesting' and 'just as interesting as psychiatric knowledge' (Abbott, 1995, p 548). He spent a time seeing the history of professions as 'a history of turf wars' (p 552) and social work as shaped by conflict over boundaries.

The standard account of the formation of social work views the profession as arising out of a turf competition between the charity organization societies with their 'scientific' ethos of casework, and the settlements with their chaotically comprehensive services and their broad social agenda. The view is that the settlements more or less lost out to the new scientism of Mary Richmond and others. The settlements' broad interests in reform and preventative services were replaced by the narrow, vocational, casework-centered approach of the social work schools. (p 556)

Over against this he argues that in the various sub-areas like probation and family work 'boundaries began to emerge between different kinds of people doing the same kinds of work, or between different styles of work with roughly similar clients, or between one kind of workplace and another.... They were not boundaries *of* anything but, rather, simple locations of difference' (p 557). 'Thus, I come to the notion that social entities actually emerge from boundaries' (p 558).[12]

Michael Bloor

The British sociologist Michael Bloor is of interest for different reasons, and for how he repeatedly prods at the way sociologists, especially through their methodological practices, ought to be of value. He argues that 'the real opportunities for sociological influence lie closer to the coalface than they do to head office' and that they lie in 'relations with practitioners, not with the managers of practice' (Bloor, 1997, p 234).

In reviews of a street ethnography of HIV-related risk behaviour among Glasgow male prostitutes, and comparative ethnographies of eight therapeutic communities, he suggests there are two ways in which ethnography might speak to the practitioner. First, it may 'model' a service delivery that can be transferred to service providers. For example, 'ethnographic fieldwork, in its protracted and regular contacts with research subjects, has much in common with services outreach work' (p 227). From his therapeutic community studies, Bloor suggests the very act of comparative judgement can model helpful service practice. 'Rich description of particular kinds of therapeutic practice can assist practitioners in making evaluative judgements about their own practices' (p 229). Second, ethnographers may, where

---

[12] I realise that readers will be aware that Abbott's work on professions also has relevance to social work (Abbott, 1988).

appropriate, draw practitioners' attention to practices they think worth dissemination and further consideration. Bloor and McKeganey listed seven practices that seemed to them to promote therapy in their original settings (Bloor and McKeganey, 1989), and which they discussed with the practitioners in the therapeutic communities. Incidentally, they point out the corresponding implications for ethnographers, in that:

> any attempts to further exploit the evaluative potential of ethnography for a practitioner audience must be paralleled by a growth in ethnographic studies which focus on practitioners' work, not practitioners' conduct. (Bloor and McKeganey, 1989, p 210)

Until that time, when 'citizens themselves commend the work of practitioners, then it is not the place of sociologists to murmur of false consciousness and demand resistance to pastoral care' (Bloor, 1997, p 235). In a deceptively gentle later piece, Bloor concurs with and illustrates that the researcher has an obligation to bring about good.

> It is an obligation we all share in all social settings and that therefore stretches across the entire duration of a research project. And it is not an obligation we can ignore with impunity in the service of some higher calling such as scientific rigour. (Bloor, 2010, p 20)

Stephen Turner

Turner's interest takes us full circle to early Chicago social programmes and sociology (Turner, 1996). Reflecting on the Pittsburgh Survey – dismissed as part of the larger survey movement by Faris (1967) – he draws on early texts that 'give shape to a kind of dim memory of a movement to promote social reform through social research, which, for mysterious reasons, disappeared' (Turner, 1996, p 35). He locates it in 'a history of expertise'.

The Pittsburgh Survey involved Paul Kellogg and the Russell Sage Foundation closely associated with the New York City Charity Organization Society. Kellogg's idea of the survey was one based on the social worker as an engineer to achieve comprehensive community reform. He presented social workers as experts with the kind of diagnostic powers that a physician acquires, bringing in expertise that by its nature is external to the local situation – an expertise on human needs.

This optimistic vision was never realised. Indeed, even within the Russell Sage Foundation there were frictions about this issue. Mary Richmond, for example, was critical of gathering data for publicity rather than by a spirit of discovery. Individual therapy rather than community reform emerged as the dominant model in social work as it became professionalised. But Turner's analysis revisits historical movements to find them interesting in the context of a wider issue that has, and will be, a perennial concern for social work – the nature of the claims to expertise that ought to and plausibly may be made.

Daniel Cefai

The French sociologist Daniel Cefai has extensive work that is empirically informed and theorised regarding central aspects of social work. One of his current interests is in the idea of a sociology of valuation and evaluation, drawing on the ideas of the philosopher John Dewey. A useful starting point for how he develops this understanding can be seen in his article on outreach work in Paris (Cefai, 2015).[13]

Jaber Gubrium

Gubrium's work probably is generally more widely known than that of the others included here. His collaboration with Holstein has yielded some excellent work on methodology (for example, Holstein and Gubrium, 1995). But he has persistently followed his interest in – as he expresses it – the social organisation of care and treatment in human service institutions. His work extends from the 1970s on the everyday practice of caregiving in nursing homes through to a co-edited book on *Reimagining the human service relationship* (Gubrium et al, 2016). This book explores how the move toward greater efficiency and accountability in the human services has weakened the bond between users and providers, and rethinks traditional networks of exchange so that professionals can find new ways to foster trust and collaboration within modern management strategies. Gubrium's 1989 piece on 'The descriptive tyranny of forms' has been widely read by social workers and can be downloaded from his home page.[14] In the introduction to the 2016 book, he writes:

---

[13] Links to some of his work can be seen at http://ehess.academia.edu/DanielCefa%C3%AF and http://cems.ehess.fr/index.php?2528.

[14] http://sociology.missouri.edu/faculty/gubrium.shtml

The everyday lives of insiders (and professionals) are as saturated by the vagueness and noticings of troubles, both their own and those of users, as they are beholden to the logic of clearly seeing, and seeing to, the problems over which they have formal oversight. (p 21)

Methodological practice

Continuing this exploration, spanning almost a century, the final new point I want to make in this chapter is about how there is the possibility for the rich transfer of practice between sociology and social work in terms of methods of understanding and inquiry. I have spent much of my career thinking and writing about this question (compare Shaw, 2011), but here I introduce the work of three others by way of closure for this chapter.

Walter Reckless

The Chicago School again yields a helpful starting point. Walter Reckless was a contemporary of Thrasher. We met him in passing earlier in this chapter, recalling and regretting the way social work, as a field of professional study, was marginalised in the minds of some of his contemporaries. He, along with Thrasher and others, was pursuing his doctoral studies in that remarkable period of intellectual fertility. Reckless is of interest as much for his observation on method as for the substance of his research. He has much to say about case study, including first-hand life histories. His article on 'Suggestions for the sociological study of problem children' (1928) carried an extended section on the questions he suggests should be part of case study. When he reaches the 'sociological study', he has a footnote saying: 'The suggested questions covering the child's world as he sees it are framed purposely in language he is able to understand' (Reckless, 1928, p 162). Examples from a long list include:

> Where would you rather live than on the street where your family lives at present? Why? What's the best thing about your neighborhood? What don't you like about your neighborhood? Why? What wrong goings-on do you know about in your neighborhood? What's the worst thing you know about that goes on in the neighborhood?....' (pp 162 onwards)

On recording, he says: 'The sociological interviews should be recorded as nearly verbatim as possible'. Burgess had much to say on this same point (for example, Burgess, 1928). Reckless insists:

> The test of validity of those scientific techniques which have taken upon themselves the task of penetrating the mysteries of child life, is not that they should be painfully exact but that they should throw light on the problems at hand. But no matter whether the expert has a psychiatric or a sociological technique, he must approach the problem child through the avenue of the individual case study in order to get the proper focus on him. When a case is properly studied, it should be a 'close up' of a person – an intimate and revealing picture of him and his back-ground. (Reckless, 1928, p 156)

He means more by the word 'picture' than may be imagined, adopting the delightful expression 'sociological photography':

> The sociological photography of children is not proposed to displace the psychiatric technique but rather to round out case studies which ideally should consist of medical and psychological examinations, a psychiatric diagnosis, and a sociological investigation. (pp 156-7)

In this, 'The subjective data are perhaps the most revealing of all. For they disclose the ways in which the child responds to his "surroundings" and consequently help to delimit his world and the conditions which affect him' (p 166).

In the following year, Reckless reported the application of this approach to the placement and study of foster children, in which he remarked how the case study was 'built around the objective (although qualitative) observations of the child in the free-play situation' (Reckless, 1929, p 569).

Pauline Young

Between the two world wars, it was Pauline Young more than others who elaborated the direct intervention consequences of their sociological thinking. It is worth emphasising how Young, along with the remarkable Ada Sheffield, expounded the conjunction between sociology and social work. Whereas the dominant convention, to this day, is for social workers to set out the value of research findings as a practice *resource*, Young and Sheffield talk primarily in terms of the value for practice of sociological *method*.

Young made her contribution especially in the field of reflections on interviewing. As early as 1928, social workers were producing work that the sociologist Ray Lee describes as 'the early development of a – to modern eyes – quite sophisticated understanding of interview practice by social workers in the United States' (Lee, 2008, p 291). Pauline Young's book on social work interviewing – significantly subtitled *A sociological analysis* – is unambiguously a practice text. Yet she speaks in a voice strange to social work, now as much as at any time. It is her constant easy movement between what today would be seen as different even dissonant literatures that is so striking. Interviewing, she insists, 'is itself a phenomenon in the general field of social interaction, and the problems which it faces have to do for the most part with social situations' (Young, 1935, p x) and a large proportion of the material on which she draws comes out of disciplines other than social work.

Young observes at one point:

> The research interview is more concerned with the analysis of the fundamental processes involved in social situations, social problems and human behavior than with their diagnosis. The research interview, as such, has little or no immediate interest in practical problems and does not undertake to find solutions for them. (1935, p 36)

This at first glance seems to make a traditional dichotomy between social work interviews and research interviews, but the subsequent context makes this difficult to sustain. She is not talking about interviews that researchers do, but more about an orientation towards interviewing, and notes that it is not the case that any interview is just one or the other. Most important, she is working through the different kinds of *social work* interview. She discusses kinds of knowledge – for her they are 'spatial or material' and 'social and personal' – and has eight tests of a successful interview that entail assumptions far distant from the psychiatric hegemony of some of the social work schools:

> Have I rendered the interviewee articulate...?
> Have I seen and understood the interviewee's problems and position from his point of view?
> Have I succeeded in learning his attitudes...?
> Did I enter his life?

> Have I enlarged his social world...?
> Have I invaded the personality of the interviewee or secured
> his story against his will or his knowledge?
> Did I secure important data...?
> Did I learn the cause of his behavior?
> Did I impose my views or plans...? (Young, 1935, pp 85-6)

Her sociologically driven social work practice is worked out in an earlier article with Erle Young, titled 'Getting at the boy himself: through the personal interview' (Young and Young, 1928). They say of boys:

> Scores of correlated and uncorrelated facts are known about
> them. The thing, however, about which we know least is
> the boy *himself*.... In short, we know the boy's external
> characteristics but not his personal and intimate life. To
> learn that we must gain access into the world in which he
> lives and in which he has his being.... He cannot be studied
> or understood apart from this world. (Young and Young,
> 1928, p 409; emphasis in original)

We already have seen her remark earlier in this book that 'common language must be rooted in common experiences; "facts are *facts* only in a world of discourse"' (Young, 1928/1929, p 499; emphasis in original). Through two life-history case studies, Young and Young conclude that the boy and the city 'are two aspects of a single process. They represent an intimate relationship of two interacting forces' (p 412).

The authors make an interesting connection between interviewing and intervention when they say:

> Just as the formal methods of interviewing ordinarily
> employed in social case work fail to get to the inner story
> of the boy, so formal methods of discipline fail to reform
> him since they are not based on sympathetic insight.... The
> informal interview method may be used as a therapeutic
> device and may be made the starting point for social
> reconstruction. (Young and Young, 1928, p 414)

They argue the implications for how service interventions are structured in concluding that the agencies of society do not respond to boys as a whole:

The social problems presented by the boy are not due to the fact that the city lacks mechanisms for the social control of boys but rather that there is such a multiplicity of social controls. (p 413)

Gerhard Riemann

Gerhard Riemann's work on ethnographies of practice has been carried out with social work students in Germany. His approach includes asking students to keep ethnographic field notes. He gives a helpful instance of a student ethnographic note that I reproduce here, knowing that exemplifying ethnographic field notes is better than suggesting rules for their construction (Riemann, 2005, p 93). The experience is commonplace. A student is arriving on day one for a practice placement:

> This is probably the first client I have met here. He looks insecure. He has thrown away his cigarette and is constantly fumbling with a piece of paper that is in a transparent folder. I greet him by saying, 'hello'. We grin at each other. He does not say anything. While I am still thinking if and how I should start a conversation with him, he says, 'Hi, are you also here because of the bill?' I must certainly look somewhat puzzled. I do not know at all what kind of 'bill' could be meant. He probably realises my bewilderment, and he looks in another direction. I say, 'No, I am not here because of the bill. I am on a work placement with the social workers of the clinic for the next few weeks and I am supposed to start today. I have been waiting for Mrs K. for quite some time.' I feel somewhat strange as we try to establish contact—he is leaning on the door while I am sitting on the lawn. I don't like 'looking up' to him while talking to him. 'Oh, I see, uhm' is his response. Besides that I am slowly realising that he really thinks I am a CLIENT. On the one hand I think, 'That's terrible!' On the other hand I think, 'Well, that's clear. Why not?' I stand up and look at my watch. It's already 8.20 a.m. I am gazing at the young man again and discover (from the corner of my eye) a woman approaching who is in her 40s. Is this my practice teacher? No, I don't think so. She is also holding a piece of paper in her hand. Does it also have something to do with this bill? The woman comes closer, she greets him and says,

'Today I will be discharged!' She turns to me and asks, 'Are you having to stay here for long? I cannot remember you at all.' 'She also thinks of me as someone who is from here,' flashes through my mind. This has never happened to me before. Why not?....

It is worth pausing and thinking at this point, to avoid taking the mundane for granted and skipping past the puzzling. What is this social worker learning – implicitly or explicitly – from this field note? At least four issues are raised:

- the prevalence of unplanned incidents and how we respond to them;
- the nature of stigma;
- the ambiguous processes of becoming familiar with local circumstances of the clinic; and
- the occurrence of incongruity.

It is precisely an ethnographic stance that brings these to the foreground.

We have merely suggested a few cameos of how this argument for a methodological social work practice may be developed. It should be read in conjunction with Bloor's suggestion earlier in this chapter that ethnography and the act of comparative judgement might model a form of service delivery, and the brief passage on interviews and spatial understanding in Chapter Six, where the examples also readily facilitate translation to social work practice.

Making practical sense

We have distinguished in various ways how we might explain the relationship between social work and sociology as a form of practice. In consequence, it:

- prompts us to think hard about social work;
- makes us reflect on the nature, boundaries and social dynamics of the social work research community;
- surprises us through fresh light on familiar themes;
- obliges us to notice those sociologists who are doing work that, potentially at least, has something to say about social work;
- compels us to notice those of our social work colleagues who are doing interesting work informed by and speaking to sociology.

But here we reach the central question of our final chapter – what do we mean when we speak of doing good social work research? To that question we now turn.

EIGHT

Doing good social work research

After setting out the tensions and challenges endemic to social work research, I will spend a substantial part of this chapter looking at what we may learn from social work controversies. I will develop in detail one area, perhaps unfamiliar to readers, where dispute and debate has occurred, and draw conclusions regarding how we ought to manage controversy. Finally, I will touch on three general topics:

- The essential limits of science in social work.
- The misuses of science.
- The principles and practices that help foster good social work research.

What obligations are we under as human beings when we carry out research? What moral, ethical and social standards and values should both constrain and enrich our work? Are there risks and threats posed by the character of the research enterprise? What might we be asserting if we refer to a belief in a unity of vision and purpose in research? I have expressed these questions without specific reference to social work because they are by and large shared across all disciplines and fields of planned and systematic inquiry. This assumption is reflected through this final chapter – and throughout the book – in the quotations drawn from scientists of various hues. But taken together, they are what I have in mind by posing the question of 'good' social work research.

Invited to judge if a particular example of social work research is good or not, one is likely to assume the question is about whether intelligent and appropriate decisions were made about the study design, the methodology, the analysis and interpretation of the data, and so on. The direct research experience the majority of social workers have of carrying out research may be related to small projects linked to time on qualifying programmes, when it is precisely these criteria by which their work will have been assessed. In addition, this will be viewed in the light of how adequately a given project reflects and advances social work values. Arising out of such judgements questions may be raised regarding how commitments to, for example, rigour or justice have and ought to have been weighted and related. Is one more important than the other?

These all are matters that we dealt with in the first two chapters of the book. While Chapters One, Two and Eight can be read as a whole, the main concerns of this final chapter lie behind those we have delved into already. What then do we have in mind in wondering about 'good' social work research? To pose the questions in the opening paragraph helps to bring together the more general challenges and inevitable tensions that are part and parcel of social work and research, and which have cropped up throughout this book.

Tensions and challenges

We recognised early in this book that social workers and their associated research community members are not hermetically sealed from life in general, and that foreseen and unforeseen factors such as climate change, terrorism, a lifelong disability after being knocked from a bicycle, economic recession, being turned out of your family home in the Indian sub-continent after changing faith, an earthquake in Nepal, and much else, all pattern and sometimes radically shift the direction of lives. In these wider contexts, career and discipline considerations may seem relatively mundane. But they are present nonetheless, and endemic in any effort to practice good social work research.

The challenge of local and national research environments and cultures overlaps but is distinguishable from country to country. In addition, in any one country there will be ebbs and flows. Research environments in which we work may prove supportive or not. External expectations regarding the role of universities in contemporary society filter through, as through government demands, especially in the West, for measurable 'impact'. There often is healthy scepticism about the role of universities and their relation to government. I came across the following in the national History Museum in Hanoi.[1]

> To establish the nation, study is first. To control the nation, talented people are important. When the country was in danger from invaders, people did not pay much attention to study, so talented people were limited.
>
> Oh! To end disorder is control, thus it is necessary to set up examinations to replace disorder with control.

[1] Tày Son Dynasty 15 Year of the reign of Quang Trung (1790), A Decree on Building Schools.

The frequent subordination of social work as a professional and disciplinary category to some wider category may push social work research closer to some fields and more distant from others. Social work is small and so may for funding purposes be subsumed under or brought into varying degrees of helpful association with a wider category, whether it be health policy, social care, or human services.

Disciplinary insularity is a temptation in perhaps all disciplines. In the previous chapter, we cautioned against a chronic tendency, in the US as much as anywhere, to a socially inward focus. There are structure and identity elements to this, which include the 'placing' of social work in universities and whether social work is seen as belonging at or 'below' university level. The significance of late research career entry plays a part here. In the UK at least, it is rare for social work academic careers to start before someone is perhaps into their late thirties. The important underlying consideration is that of the relationship between the professional and the scholarly.

We touched briefly in Chapter Five on the steady growth of specialisation in the university world, and how the individual achieves by being, in Weber's expression, 'a strict specialist'. That the career in the academy is always a hazard was a central emphasis of Weber's speech a century ago (Weber, 1948 [1919], p 134). One needs, he believed, to have a calling for research. It is a necessity to have a personality, one's 'own voice', to be a true academic researcher. Without a personal voice, one ends up as a specialist only, rather than a true academic researcher. Fuller's prescription is to present the task of education as to release the specialist insights of research 'in to larger social settings, and not to reinforce their original theoretical packaging by treating students as if they were potential recruits to specialist ranks' (Fuller, 2009, p 30). Burawoy, in his now famous advocacy of public sociology, considered in Chapter Two, was not speaking for social work, but a straight substitution of 'social work' for 'sociology' would not go amiss. 'If our predecessors set out to change the world we have too often ended up conserving it. Fighting for a place in the academic sun, sociology developed its own specialized knowledge….' (Burawoy, 2005, p 5).

There are a number of challenges that flow more immediately from the research practice. These include a relative absence of research communities and networks. I think a distinction is needed between **social** networking and **scholarly** networking – though the two are, of course, closely linked. Then there is the challenge of research skills and competencies. There are two possible problems of **superficiality** and **limited diversity**. Methods are too often treated in an instrumental way – as necessary means to an end, but not of interest as such.

Understanding, keeping up with and exploiting technological change is a further challenge. We should avoid being too now-focused when thinking about 'new' technology. However, it *is* a challenge. It also relates to the wider work on the place of technology in society – a strand that goes back at least to the French social theorist Jacques Ellul. While there are new *forms* of technology, the phrase 'new technology' may be misleading. What we think of as 'new' is not essentially so, but only so at this moment in our time. As Karen Staller says when talking about this topic, 'the future quickly becomes the past and that which is cutting edge today will be – someday soon – antiquated' (Staller, 2010, p 287). If I had told my social work students in the 1990s that email – that new and exciting possibility – would 20 years later begin to be seen as the province of an older generation, they would have mocked in disbelief. This pattern of change is partly because 'the way we collect, retrieve, store and manage data will always be shaped by context including the historic moment, and our relationship to it' (Staller, 2010, p 287).

Finally, the democratisation of social research in general and social work research in particular is a constant incentive to reflection. Social work stands out among the social sciences, in that for most in other fields this is a question of collaboration and participation rather than anything more radical, such as user-led research. For some, this is a challenge that in one way is simple, if hugely demanding: how to more or less radically deliver on the democratisation of research. For others, it is a challenge of how to respond to the question mentioned above of weighing and counter-weighing rigour and justice.

Task Box 8.1: Technological change

Can you trace the key moments in your developing response to technological change in social work?

Disagreements and controversies

Is social work marked by controversies? The question may seem naïve, but it reminds us of the need to be clear about just what is being said. Once one looks for discussion of the question, it appears that the nature of controversies is too little considered in social work. This is due in part to how the rationalist tradition, by its assumptions, sees controversies as abnormal, deviant phenomena. The position I take is that the occurrence of controversies is not a question of error but 'an indicator of ... deep-rooted tensions which go to the very heart of science, both with regard to its character and function' (Brante and Elzinga, 1990, p 35). We should value our controversies while thinking as carefully as we can about the issues involved. Latour presents controversies as a tug or war. On one side, we have radicals and those he calls progressists; on the other, reactionaries and conservatives.

- Radical: scientific knowledge is constructed entirely out of social relations.
- Progressist: science is partly constructed out of social relations, but nature somehow 'leaks in' at the end.
- Conservatives: although science escapes from society there are still factors from society that 'leak in' and influence its development.
- Reactionaries: science becomes scientific only when it finally sheds any trace of social construction.

'Radical' and 'reactionary' correspond to the poles subject and object, with a constant battle to occupy a position closer to one or other pole and to use one pole to explain the other (Latour, 1992). Different types of controversies occur, because there are different kinds of conflicts. These may be with regard to facts, theory or principle. I want to try thinking of this in relation to an example and one I suspect will be less familiar to readers. It is about a difference on a range of positions between Donald Campbell and Lee Cronbach. Getting our teeth into the nuances of the arguments is among the more demanding sections of this book, but well repays the investment.

Donald Campbell

Donald Campbell (1916-96) gave this third-person description of himself: 'Campbell is a social psychologist turned research methodologist and lately theorist of science. He accepts epistemological relativism but stops short of ontological nihilism' (Campbell, 1981, p 486). Partly through his influence, it was widely assumed in the 1960s that experimental designs to measure the outcomes of innovative programmes were the benchmark and critical test for *all* evaluation. Campbell coined the term 'internal validity' to refer to inferences about the relationship between independent and dependent variables. He gives greater weight to internal validity than to external validity. Of what use, he would argue, is generalising a relationship if one doubts the relationship itself?

He was a critical realist, accepting the existence of a real world beyond knowers, yet vigorously criticising the slightest trace of naïve realism that assumes our observations or theories directly mirror reality. His emphasis on the logical impossibility of induction, and the primacy of falsification methods in justifying claims to knowledge, linked to his critical realism, all reveal his debt to the philosopher Karl Popper.

Campbell drew on his own early work on cultural differences in levels of susceptibility to optical illusions, to explore ways in which cross-cultural failures of communication might be distinguished from cross-cultural *perceptual* differences. He thought it was extremely difficult to ascertain whether the members of different cultures perceive things differently (Campbell, 1964). Reflecting on this research more than 30 years later, he insisted that 'to interpret as a cultural difference what is in reality a failure of communication [is] the most ubiquitous source of error in efforts to know the other' (Campbell, 1996, p 165). However, he does not believe that such difficulties are insurmountable. 'Those who make knowing the other problematic are correct. Those who regard it as impossible to any degree are wrong' (p 169). Thus he rejects relativists ('ontological nihilists' is his term) and 'other more recent imports from the cafes of Paris' (1996, p 159). He thus maintains a double-edged epistemology, emphasising both the inevitability of doubt and the belief that we can overcome this to a practically useful degree and know the other. His evolutionary philosophy undergirded his epistemology.

This deals with only one broad area of Campbell's thinking. For example, the ethnographer Howard Becker taught with Campbell between 1960 and 1979 and was a major influence on two essays written by Campbell in the 1970s (Campbell, 1978, 1979). Campbell came to accept Becker's critiques of standard quantitative social science as 'valid and extremely relevant' (Campbell, 1996, p 161), and criticised quantitative scientists who 'under the influence of missionaries from logical positivism, presume that in true science, quantitative knowing replaces qualitative, common-sense knowing' (Campbell, 1979, p 50). He regards qualitative knowing as both the test and the building block of quantitative knowing:

> This is not to say that such common-sense naturalistic observation is objective, dependable or unbiased. But it is all that we have. It is the only route to knowledge – noisy, fallible and biased though it be. (Campbell, 1979, p 54)

His second contribution to qualitative research was through raising the question of whether qualitative methods can fulfil the same cause-probing purpose as quantitative methods. He uses the analogue of experimental research to suggest ways of strengthening case studies and 'constructs one of the strongest cases to date that qualitative methods can yield valid causal knowledge' (Shadish et al, 1990, p 135). He later observed that, 'in addition to the quantitative and quasi-experimental case study approach ... our social science armamentarium also needs a humanistic, validity-seeking, case study method' (Campbell, 1994, p x).

Lee Cronbach

Turning to a much less well-known scholar, Lee Cronbach (1916-2001) is one of the most important and least appreciated theorists. His work is almost never cited in social work literature, and except in the major review by Shadish and colleagues (1990), his work is only drawn on occasionally and selectively even in the American literature. Yet the work of this 'tough-minded master of conceptual distinctions' (Scriven, 1986, p 15) is:

> a brilliant *tour de force*, unusually rewarding if closely read, trenchant in analysis of the *status quo*, and creating truly unique alternatives sensitive to the scholarly need for general knowledge and the practitioner need for local application. (Shadish et al, 1990, p 375; emphasis in original)

The key phrases in his vocabulary are external validity, formative evaluation, causation, generalisation and pluralist methodology. We have seen that the motifs of Campbell's approach are inference from the internal validity of evaluations, and assessment of outcomes through summative comparisons of alternative programmes. Cronbach gave priority to neither of these. Against Campbell he argues the priority of *external* validity and *formative* evaluation – evaluation *within* and not *between* programmes.

At the core of Cronbach's position is the claim that '"external validity" – validity of inferences that go beyond the data – is the crux of social action, not "internal validity"' (Cronbach et al, 1980, p 231). Behind this lies a particular view of causation. For Campbell, internal validity is about the relationship between interventions and outcomes in a given random sample. Cronbach considers this concept insignificant: 'Campbell's writings make internal validity a property of trivial, past tense, and local statements' (Cronbach, 1982, p 137).

Cronbach prioritises the understanding and explanation of mechanisms operating in a local context, in order that plausible inferences can be drawn regarding other settings, people and interventions that are of interest to policy makers. It is extrapolation that matters – 'a prediction about what will be observed in a study where the subjects or operations depart in some respect from the original study' (Cronbach, 1986, p 94). It is not 'before-and-after', but 'during–during–during', as he somewhere says.

To achieve this local, contextualised understanding, he rejects the notion of evaluation in which 'the program is to "play statue" while the evaluator's slow film records its picture' (Cronbach et al, 1980, p 56) in favour of case studies drawing primarily but not exclusively on qualitative methods. He insists many times on the need for 'flexible attack' and 'does not want a particular conception of scientific methods to trivialise the process of asking important questions' (Shadish et al, 1990, p 349). 'Planning inquiry ... is the art of recognising tradeoffs and placing bets' (Cronbach, 1986, p 103).

His pluralist view of methodology echoes his conception of the policy context in which evaluation is located. With characteristic dry wit he remarks, 'The very proposal to evaluate has political impact. To ask about the virtue of Caesar's wife is to suggest she is not above suspicion' (Cronbach et al, 1980, p 163). Cronbach and his colleagues complain that evaluation theory has 'been developed almost wholly around the image of command' and the assumption that managers and policy makers have a firm grip on the controls of decision making. However, 'most action is determined by a pluralistic community not by a lone decision-maker' (Cronbach et al, 1980, p 84). Hence, evaluation enters a context of governance that is typically one of accommodation rather than command. 'A theory of evaluation must be as much a theory of political interaction as it is a theory of how knowledge is constructed' (Cronbach et al, 1980, pp 52-3).

Having allowed that decisions rarely hinge solely on the empirical evidence, Cronbach is ready to trade off precision ('fidelity') against relevance ('bandwidth'). He is hostile towards both goal-setting models of evaluation, and evaluation as accountability: 'We are uneasy about the close association of evaluation with accountability. In many of its uses the word becomes an incantation and one that can cast a malign spell' (Cronbach et al, 1980, p 133). He regards the role of the evaluator as a multi-partisan advocate. While the evaluator may serve some partisan interest, 'his unique contribution is a critical, scholarly cast of mind' (p 67). He sees evaluation within a context of political accommodation as both conservative and committed to change.

> To be meliorist is the evaluator's calling. Rarely or never will evaluative work bring a 180-degree turn in social thought. Evaluation assists in piecemeal adaptations: perhaps it does tend to keep the *status* very nearly *quo*. (Cronbach et al, 1980, p 157; emphasis in original)

There are problematic aspects to Cronbach's theory. His concern with large-scale policy and programme evaluation makes his ideas less readily transferable to evaluation of local projects and practices. His pluralist political stance was fashioned prior to the advent of right-wing market policies and will be unacceptable to some readers. Finally, his arguments may be too complex to provide the methods for practice that most evaluators seek. Yet his influence has already proved diverse, and his work has extensive implications for key aspects of evaluation, including generalisation, causal explanations, multi-site case studies, and the policy relevance of evaluation.

Reflections

One reason for introducing Cronbach and Campbell in their relation to one another – apart from the intrinsic significance of the issues with which they dealt – is to demonstrate how controversy acts not as a difficulty or unfortunate problem, but as a valuable anvil on which important issues can be hammered into intellectual and practical shape. Having suggested that this is but one kind of controversy, I do not want to say more about their nature, but keep to our theme and ask, 'How ought we to handle disagreements between us?' in ways that make dignity and worth possible. Three kinds of work are needed – empirical, cognitive and social.

Kirk and Reid correctly stress the need for treating questions of science *empirically* (Kirk and Reid, 2002). Empirically we may seek to grasp how contending claims for jurisdiction over a specific field or problem arise; who is regarded as having the right to speak; who is the real expert; how to understand alliance seeking and how resources are mobilised; and how controversies may be resolved or at least find some kind of termination.

Cognitively, I would advocate three stances, beginning with the value of a falsifying perspective. 'It will incline people to accept criticism, state their claims with clarity, cast their research design in fruitful ways, open their theories and hypotheses to empirical test…' (Phillips, 2000, p 141). Phillips laments, in terms that have a measure of force, that 'the tendency to search for "confirming" rather than disconfirming or refuting evidence is particularly strong in research that uses qualitative methods' (2000, p 144) and is often marked by a 'mental set' that directs the observations. I would not be overly dogmatic on this. Gerald Holton, a physicist and historian, did not think that was the task of the individual in relation to one's own work, but the responsibility of the scientific community' (Wolpert and Richards, 1997, p 190). So Popper's principle 'does not work in everyday science as a mandate upon the scientist himself or herself, especially in the early stage of work. But it is perfectly usual for the community as a whole to take up that task' (Wolpert and Richards, 1997, p 191). Second, we should retain, despite the manifold difficulties it brings, the distinction between rational and social causes in science, between epistemic and non-epistemic criteria for good social work science and research. Third, there are real controversies in social work science, and they never can be restricted to rational, cognitive issues.

In *social* terms, practitioners of social work science should avoid sentimentality, and adopt a moderate scepticism, especially about their own work. Does (moderate) scepticism lead to paralysed inaction? Not necessarily. It is possible to be philosophically sceptical yet practically committed to action.

I am uncomfortable with how disagreements often are conducted in social work. There is a too-frequent tendency to resort to what Raymond Williams called 'swearing' (Williams, 1983). We commence in attack mode. In addition, we too rarely source arguments in the writings of those who are proponents of that with which we disagree, and too often take as adequate the work of those with whom we are sympathetic. There is also a tendency to voice positions by a reductionist analysis of those with whom we disagree.

Contrary to this, I assume that we can – and probably must – talk *with* (not *at*) those with whom we profoundly disagree, on the assumption that in principle we can hear each other, and that we should respect and assume that their positions are held with integrity and have as much right to be heard as our own. In accord with this, I have long taken the rather challenging approach (for me) of asking people with whom I deeply disagree to comment critically on my draft papers. I spend much time thinking what I am walling in or walling out. I have remarked somewhere that, in common with Robert Frost in his much anthologised poem, 'Mending Wall', I have no time for hunters who leave 'not one stone on a stone … to please the yelping dogs'. I do aspire to provoke conversation and debate. I doubt it would make consistent sense to do any of this if I believed that those with whom I disagreed lived in another paradigmatic world.

These are all areas where debate and difference exist. I am too often disappointed by the way the social work community handles differences. One point of reference may be the following principles set out by Hammersley (1995):

- The overriding concern should be the truth of claims, and not their political or practical consequences.
- Arguments should be judged solely on the grounds of their plausibility and credibility, and not on the grounds of the personal characteristics of those advancing the argument.
- Researchers should be willing to change their views, and should behave as if other researchers are also so willing, at least until there is strong counter-evidence. This requires Romm's plea for the 'acceptance of the need to open oneself to "bad news"' (Romm, 1995, p 158).
- Where agreement does not result, the researcher should accept there is some reasonable doubt regarding the argument they are advancing.
- There should be no restriction on participation in such discourse on political or religious grounds.

Along with such standards, we may add the need to beware some forms of science-led positions, especially when they appear to take a rationalist position that exalts reason above other forms of knowledge and understanding, and avoid the pitfall of the romanticism of positions where practice experience can always 'defeat' arguments from research. The former reflects a rationalist position whereby 'science' has inherent bragging rights over 'practice'. Practice is always viewed as something that in a responsive way must be 'based on' research; social work is viewed as standing in a beneficiary, suppliant pose towards social science. We explored this problem in Chapter Three. The chronic forms of subordination – of 'practice' to 'theory', or 'research' to 'practice' – hide how social work research has proved most fruitful when at least as much interested in what practice has to say to ideas or research as *vice versa*. 'Knowing' and 'doing', research and practice, are not two wholly distinct areas that need mechanisms to connect them, but are to a significant degree part and parcel of one another.

This suggests the value of a relationship between of knowing and doing that is something like two adjacent 'open systems'. This offers a radical contrast with, for example, the 'more or less explicit common sense assumption that sociologists are *primarily interested in analyzing* in order to comprehend the complexity of society and social relations in a generalized form, and that social work researchers are *primarily interested in intervention and changing* individuals and/or groups.'[2]

How ought we to own and take forward these agendas today? In part, perhaps, by developing interest groups in a forum such as the European Conference for Social Work Research, or by having social work groups in national or international networks hosted by other disciplines, and also by working on the nature of, for example, a 'practical' sociology – so long as it is not based on a view that what is practical is in a subordinate relation to what is theoretical. Finally, we can work jointly to set and indeed tackle an agenda for fields of work.

These are at heart pleas for a Socratic set of intellectual dispositions. They ask for empathy. To what extent do I accurately represent the viewpoints I disagree with? Can I summarise the views of my opponents to their satisfaction? Can I see insights in the views of others and prejudices in my own? Do I hold myself to the same intellectual standards I expect others to honour?

The limits of science

An important safeguard is to recognise and understand the limits to research and scientific knowledge. To recognise the limits of social work research is not the same as drawing attention to its imperfections and limitations. The advantage of thinking of the limits of research is that 'acknowledging what our field *does not know* or *cannot do* increases its credibility regarding what it *does know* and *can do*' (Grisso and Vincent, 2005, p 3; emphasisin original). Social work should be 'scientific' in several ways, and it does and should have something 'scientific' to say. Habermas has talked about forms of ideal speech in which all who participate in discourse must have equal chances to present interpretations, to make assertions, recommendations, explanations and corrections. All also must have equal chances to problematise or challenge the validity of these presentations, to make arguments for and against. This is reflected in the position taken by Ernest House, the American evaluation theorist whose position we set out in Chapter Two, who develops the example of negotiating a fair and demanding evaluation agreement (1980, chapter 8), in which all participants should meet the demanding conditions that they:

---

[2]   I am quoting at this point from correspondence from Maria Appel Nissen, emphasis in original.

- not be coerced;
- be able to argue their position;
- accept the terms under which the agreement is reached;
- negotiate – and this is not simply 'a coincidence among individual choices';
- not pay excessive attention to one's own interests;
- adopt an agreement that affects all equally;
- select a policy for evaluation that is in the interests of the group to which it applies;
- have equal and full information on relevant facts;
- avoid undue risk to participants arising from incompetent and arbitrary evaluations.

In doing so, social work scientists should recall John Madge's insistence long ago that they should not 'strain so busily after an obsolete ideal that they neglect the more pertinent aspects of their task' (Madge, 1953, p 290). They should not want to be 'glorifying uncertainty', and 'the quest for exactness cannot lightly be renounced' (p 290). Yet '[e]xact truth is both a proper objective and an unattainable one ... we have to be content with some residue of uncertainty' (p 291).

This will involve work. Foucault remarked that 'to work is to undertake to think something other than what you thought before' (cited in O'Farrell, 2005, p 45). The cultural theorist Stuart Hall said more strongly, 'I want to suggest a different metaphor for theoretical work: the metaphor of struggle, of wrestling with the angels. The only theory worth having is that which you have to fight off, not that which you speak with profound fluency' (cited in Grossberg, 1996, pp 265-6).

The misuses of research and science

The acceptance of standards suggested by Hammersley, House or anyone else would not, of course, guarantee that social work will be free of *misuses* of science. We may smile at G.K. Chesterton's remark that 'It is perfectly obvious that in any decent occupation (such as bricklaying or writing books) there are only two ways (in any special sense) of succeeding. One is by doing very good work, the other is by cheating' (cited in Bastow et al, 2014, p 37). Indeed, history is scattered with instances showing that at their worst 'scientific concepts can reinforce a vast array of dangerous or hateful political and moral agendas' (Jacob, 1992, p 495). 'There are evil ends directing actions, and there are ignoble curiosities of the understanding' (Merton, 1971, p 794). Max Born, the German Nobel physicist, writing in 1946 in the immediate aftermath of war, reflected:

> We have now a terrible responsibility. We should do nothing without thinking where it may lead to, and we cannot retire to an 'isolationism' or an ivory tower. Yet I am quite convinced that the eternal value of science lies in things remote from any applications, good or bad, in finding the truth about reality. (Quoted in Greenspan, 2005, p 267)

Medawar suggested a view of fraud that derives from the community characteristics of science. The principal cause of fraud is 'a passionate conviction of the truth of some unpopular or unaccepted doctrine … which one's colleagues must somehow be shocked into believing' (Medawar, 1984, p 32). He gives the example of Sir Cyril Burt's notorious work on the IQ of twins, to stress heredity. Leroy Hood, a biotechnologist, had a case of fraud in his laboratory that closely reflected Medawar's explanation. 'The rationalization that one of the people gave was: "Look, I knew what the answer was, I'd had difficulty getting the answer, so I put it together because I was sure and confident that this was in fact the answer." He claims he didn't really intend to deceive' (cited in Wolpert and Richards, 1997, pp 42-3).

I suspect that this is less likely to occur in social work, if only because the opportunities for categorically certain arguments are few and far between. Lewontin, an evolutionary biologist, argued in terms of a temptation that may be more directly transferable to social work. He has opposed prizes and honours, from Nobel prizes downwards:

> One of the things these elite institutions do is to make sure that people spend their lives – motivated by the desire for fame and for elite status – working on problems that they can solve and get famous by…. My pleasure in science, I would say, is exactly what every scientist says; my pleasure in science is finding out something that's true. My claim is that most of them are not telling the truth. That most of their pleasure in science comes out not from knowing what's true, but from claiming something that other people think is grand. (in Wolpert and Richards, 1997, p 110)

Jerrim and de Vries link this to the lure of an influential article in a top journal in the field of quantitative policy research. While most researchers are committed to conducting and reporting honest research, they suggest questionable research practices remain an issue. Although blatant malpractice such as altering or inventing results seems rare,[3] 'These figures are much higher for less extreme forms of poor practice, such as dropping data points based on "gut feeling" or selectively reporting results' (Jerrim and de Vries, 2017, p 123). They quote one study that reported 34% of academics admitting to such practices and 70% saying their colleagues did so. Jacob is nonetheless probably right when she concludes that:

> Science can be socially framed, possess political meaning, and also occasionally be sufficiently true, or less false, in such a way that we cherish its findings. The challenge comes in trying to understand how knowledge worth preserving occurs in time, possesses deep social relations, and can also be progressive ... and seen to be worthy of preservation. (Jacob, 1992, p 501)

Good quality in social work research

Having reflected on some of the big questions regarding social work research, here and in the opening chapters, is it possible to draw conclusions and inferences that may act as a reference point? How should we make judgements about the merits and quality of social work research?

Task Box 8.2: Your 'good' research

Some of the task boxes assume the reader is a practitioner. But assuming you are a researcher, identify an example of your research that you believe can be defended before others as good research. What is it about your research that you think justifies your claim?

When researchers talk about their work, claims of quality tend to be of two general kinds. First are *intrinsic* signifiers of quality that form around methodological and epistemological criteria. Was it rigorous, conceptually lucid, methodologically transparent, and so on? We referred earlier to a discussion of the limitations of quantitative social

---

[3] When asked about such practices among research colleagues, however, they cite one study that yielded a figure of 14%.

science as a basis for public policy. Jerrim and de Vries draw together their conclusions in terms that illustrate how such intrinsic signifiers might be developed. They say that ideally such research should:

- be independently verifiable;
- clearly communicate the uncertainty associated with any given result;
- be free from publication and media bias;
- be subject to a clear, consistent, and transparent quality-assurance process (Jerrim and de Vries, 2017, p 128).

They concede that it is 'perhaps unreasonable to expect all the above ambitions to be achieved in the near future' (p 129).

Second, quality judgments are made that draw on criteria that are *extrinsic* to the research. These include responses of the wider social work community in the form of impact, peer reviews or the community's receptiveness to a piece of work.

Rather than talk in a formal, community-standards kind of way (I have done that several times during this book), at this point I want to introduce a series of comments that were made during a research study some years ago (Shaw and Norton, 2007), in which social work researchers from a number of different universities in the UK were invited to talk about an example of their own research that they thought could be regarded as good research. What was it that led them to make this judgement? The extracts in Box 8.1 show how quite different factors were given weight from one researcher to another, in ways that suggest any simple blanket standard or rule is unlikely to work easily.

Box 8.1: Social work researchers talk about assessing the quality of their research

'In other words you're almost philosophising when you come to any research project ... why should I approach it in this particular way? Why should I use this methodology?'

'... in order to carry out this study I had to do reliability and validity tests, develop, design and develop [an] ... instrument in order to carry it out'.

'... you want to involve service users but the way that you have set it up and the methodology you intend to use and the design isn't going to work so you have to be pragmatic'.

'I suppose ... as measured against established benchmarks of quality it might be something that doesn't reach the sort of standards you would want, but because you're trying to push at the boundaries you accept a lower level of quality because you're able to open up to new areas of enquiry.'

'[The work is of good quality because it is] ... actually going to add to the debate in any way which is going to construct a better understanding.'

'... to sort of think about practical action as well as policy and theoretical concept, if they put those three things together in some way ... multiple actions that I think bring something specific about social work'.

'I didn't include partly more descriptive writings ... that doesn't in my mind have the same level as something which is more finely honed and possibly has more theoretical elements within it.'

'If I haven't worked out how what I want to say about it relates to something that I would see as a sort of improvement in human well-being then I wouldn't write the article – full stop.'

'If it's methodologically poor research that has a large impact then I would judge it as not useful because it's actually influenced moves in the wrong direction, it's added to confusion and misunderstanding and bad policy rather than the reverse.'

'Well I mean, you know, the fact that there has been all these hits on it has be, reckoned to be one of the most sort of influential articles, I suppose must say something.'

'What is the point of doing research that is stuck in a dusty journal on a library shelf and nobody ever sees it ... and this has the potential to do a lot of other positive things.'

This raises questions that are both central but not immediately tractable. Is it possible to devise a single set of criteria that encompass what some regard as incommensurable categories of inquiry? How should we judge both relevance and importance? What is socially robust research in a social work context? There are in fact four distinguishable tensions at work here:

- the question of whether some dimensions of quality judgements are more important than others;
- considerations of **rigour** versus **relevance**, inner (intrinsic) science and outer (extrinsic) science criteria (with *practice* and **theory** closely related to this);
- the response that social work should give to the various trends towards the **democratising of the research process**;
- the relationship between **perspectives** and **contexts** on the one hand and a search for **standards** against which we would wish to be accountable.

It seems to me that there are three possible general positions that are likely to shape how we respond to and seek to resolve these tensions.

- First, we may believe that some quality dimensions carry, or ought to carry, greater weight than others. This position may be adopted by those who otherwise take very different positions. For example, this may be argued from a belief that scientific knowledge always takes precedence over, for example, knowledge based on experience (hence rigour, accuracy and 'inner-science' criteria will always be more important than 'outer-science' criteria). It may also be expressed from a 'standpoint' position that the knowledge of the oppressed will always carry greater validity than that of the oppressor.
- Second, it is possible to hold a viewpoint that **quality criteria will always be contingent on local context** and the perspectives of the stakeholders, and cannot be 'assigned' in advance. Some strong postmodern positions or radical constructivist stances seem to take this view, although it is not easy to find examples where it is consistently carried through.
- Third, the position that I generally take is that **'inner'** and **'outer' science criteria** of quality **are both indispensable**, and that they should be brought to bear on any given research project or output. 'Outer-science' norms (for example, being useful or emancipatory) are neither more nor less important than 'inner-science' epistemic norms.

This may seem to be a 'having your cake and eating it' option, and one that avoids hard decisions. In an effort to develop it into a practical strategy, it starts from the deceptively simple position that quality judgments in social work research should have a set of explicit commitments. These commitments should:

- incorporate both quality-as-measured and quality-as-experienced (compare Stake and Schwandt, 2006);
- seek agreement on quality dimensions at a **middle** range of generality, with the purpose of maximising agreement between diverse epistemological positions but not requiring a unitary consensus on quality criteria;
- recognise that quality is multi-dimensional, including aspects both intrinsic and extrinsic to the research act.[4]

Furthermore we ought to commit to requiring a relatively demanding minimum demonstration of quality on all dimensions. Research quality should refer to the research product or **goal**, but also the research **process**.

These commitments are not at all straightforward to accomplish. Lying beneath them lies the ambition to develop quality standards that will 'work' for all kinds of social work and social care knowledge on the bases that there is considerable diversity of knowledge *within* social work research and that the boundaries between scientific and research knowledge and other forms of knowledge are by no means watertight.

Rules for social work radicals

I here plagiarise and slightly adapt Saul Alinsky's famous book title from almost half a century ago (Alinsky, 1971), while recalling the remark attributed to various people that 'I never prophecy about anything, especially the future.' I suspect the long-anticipated emergence of African social work scholarship will be slow. In emerging countries in Asia and South America, I also am less sure how rapidly the university social work culture will mirror economic or political power. Then again, I suspect that some strands of the picture will continue, such as evidence-based practice or at least the questions for which it stands; likewise qualitative and quantitative methods and what such questions

---

[4] Shaw and Norton (2007) spell out more fully the nature and consequences of these commitments.

signify. But here are my rules, bearing in mind I do not say we can completely escape contradiction.

i. Understand past imaginings without either adoring or despising them.

I feel the force of the words of the palaeontologist, Elwyn Simons:

> What I always tell my students is that fossils are never what you expected. It's not possible, no matter what we connive and plan and try to predict what the past was like, it's never what we thought it was going to be. (in Wolpert and Richards, 1997, p 154)

I have spent much of the last stages of my career learning the truth of this remark in exploring the history of social work in relation to what we now think of as sociology.

ii. Keep social work and life work concurrent.

A helpful way of making this kind of distinction was expressed by C. Wright Mills in his book *The sociological imagination*: 'Perhaps the most fruitful distinction with which the sociological imagination works', he suggested, 'is between "the personal troubles of milieu" and "the public issues of social structure"' (Mills, 1970, p 14). He continues:

> A trouble is a private matter: values cherished by an individual are felt by him to be threatened.... An issue is a public matter: some value cherished by publics is felt to be threatened.... [I]t is the very nature of an issue, unlike even widespread trouble, that it cannot very well be defined in terms of the immediate and everyday environments of ordinary men....
>
> The most admirable thinkers within the scholarly community you have chosen to join do not split their work from their lives. They seem to take both too seriously to allow such disassociation, and they want to use each for the enrichment of the other. (p 15)

iii. Be concerned about truth.

There are three general commitments, to a better society, truth, and some understanding of the value of science. Each of these is complex. Truth is rarely on the social science agenda. This is not to argue for absolute truth through research, but it does set a distance from postmodern positions. We are not good at doing any of these things. We often deal badly with academic disagreements. The politicisation of research is both unethical and untrue. It results in an 'evidence game' where the argument seems to be around evidence but where protagonists have no real commitment to truth. In this respect, too many social work papers are an agenda looking for some data.

iv. Cultivate a Socratic scepticism especially about positions that you hold dear.

I am convinced that a moderate Socratic scepticism is essential for social work knowledge based on evidence, understanding and justice. One does not need to be a signed-up critical theorist to believe so – though good critical theorists are sure it helps. I remarked earlier that such scepticism need not lead to paralysed inaction. It once was suggested to Foucault that his work on madness and on discipline had paralysed social workers. He would have none of it. To extend a quotation we saw in Chapter one:

> Who has been paralyzed? Do you think what I wrote on the history of psychiatry paralyzed those people who had already been concerned for some time about what was happening in psychiatric institutions?... I'm not so sure what's been said over the last fifteen years has been quite so – how shall I put it? – demobilizing.... If the social workers you are talking about don't know which way to turn, this just goes to show that they're looking, and hence are not anaesthetized or sterilized at all – on the contrary. And it's because of the need not to tie them down or immobilize them that there can be no question for me of trying to tell 'what is to be done'. If the questions posed by the social workers you spoke of are going to assume their full amplitude, the most important thing is not to bury them under the weight of prescriptive, prophetic discourse. (Foucault, 1991a, p 84)

It is possible to be philosophically sceptical yet practically committed to action. This tension between philosophy and practice is perhaps inescapable. Offstage, as it were, I would also argue that such scepticism is not incompatible with a strong affirmative faith-based position, though the rise and rise of radical Islam may make us doubt this.

Ron Walton ended a book written four decades ago by posing a question as to what social work would be like in the year 2000, saying:

> The social worker is not only a relationship technician, but what binds us, or ought to, is to be an educated and humane public servant, as sensitive in the art of administration as in casework or group work. What binds these functions of

service giving therapy and administration together is the thread of common moral principles. (Walton, 1982)

Asked whether he felt chastened with hindsight, he remarked in 2016:

> I am chastened by the thought that social welfare has been under attack from Neo-liberalism policies and weakening of social structures but heartened that social workers are still fighting in behalf of the weakest in our society and have not lost touch with the moral principles which are at the heart of social work. (Personal communication)

C. Wright Mills has on his grave an epitaph that Ralph Miliband (father of Ed Miliband, the leader of British Labour Party from 2010 to 2015) helped to choose: 'I have tried to be objective. I do not claim to be detached.'[5] Mills' final words in his book *The sociological imagination*, were as follows:

> Do not allow public issues as they are officially formulated, or troubles as they are privately felt, to determine the problems that you take up.... Above all, do not give up your moral and political autonomy by accepting in somebody else's terms the illiberal practicality of the bureaucratic ethos or the liberal practicality of the moral scatter. Know that many personal troubles cannot be solved merely as troubles, but must be understood in terms of public issues – and in terms of the problems of history making. Know that the human meaning of public issues must be revealed by relating them to personal troubles – and to the problems of the individual life. Know that the problems of social science, when adequately formulated, must include both troubles and issues, both biography and history, and the range of their intricate relations. (Mills, 1970, p 248)

Though Mills was often deeply critical of social work, his words offer a mandate for practice and research.

---

[5] These words were taken from the opening paragraphs of his last book *The Marxists*.

References

Archives

University of Chicago, Department of Sociology. Interviews with Graduate Students of the 1920s and 1930s, Special Collections Research Center, University of Chicago Library.

University of Chicago, Office of the President. Records, Special Collections Research Center, University of Chicago Library.

University of Chicago. Stuart Alfred Queen Papers, Special Collections Research Center, University of Chicago Library.

WiseARCHIVE. The Cohen Interviews: Interviews with 26 Social Work Pioneers. Interviewed by Alan Cohen c1980. University of Warwick, Modern Records Centre, www2.warwick.ac.uk/services/library/mrc/explorefurther/speakingarchives/socialwork.

References

Abbott, A, (1988) *The system of professions: An essay on the division of expert labor*, Chicago, IL: Chicago University Press.

Abbott, A. (1995) 'Boundaries of social work or social work of boundaries?', *Social Service Review*, vol 69, no 6, pp 546-62.

Abbott, E.A. (1931) *Social welfare and professional education*, Chicago, IL: University of Chicago Press.

Abse, D. (1989) *White coat, purple coat: Collected poems (1948-1988)*, London: Hutchinson.

Alinsky, S. (1971) *Rules for radicals: A pragmatic primer for realistic radicals*, New York, NY: Random House.

Allet, N., Keightley, E. and Pickering, M. (2011) 'Using self-interviews to research memory', Realities Toolkit #16, Morgan Centre for the Study of Relationships and Personal Life, University of Manchester, www.socialsciences.manchester.ac.uk/morgancentre/realities/index.html.

Atkinson, P. (2013) 'Ethnography and craft knowledge', *Qualitative Sociology Review*, vol 9, no 2, pp 56-63.

Attlee, C.R. (1920) *The Social Worker*, London: G Bell and Sons Ltd, http://archive.org/details/socialworker00attliala.

Bampton, R. and Cowton, C.J. (2002) 'The e-interview', *Forum Qualitative Sozialforschung (Forum: Qualitative Social Research)*, vol 3, no 2, http://nbn-resolving.de/urn:nbn:de:0114-fqs020295.

Bartlett, H. (1970) *The common base of social work practice*, New York, NY: National Association of Social Workers.

Bastow, S., Dunleavy, P. and Tinkler, J. (2014) *The impact of the social sciences*, London: Sage Publications.

Becker, H. (1970 [1960]) 'Notes on the concept of commitment', in H. Becker, *Sociological work*, New Brunswick, NJ: Transaction Books.

Becker, H. and Carper, J. (1970 [1956]) 'The development of identification with an occupation', in H. Becker, *Sociological work*, New Brunswick, NJ: Transaction Books.

Becker, H. and Carper, J. (1970 [1957]) 'Adjustment of conflicting expectations in the development of identification with an occupation' in H. Becker, *Sociological work*, New Brunswick, N J: Transaction Books.

Bingley, A. and Milligan, C. (2007) '"Sandplay, clay and sticks": multi-sensory research methods to explore the long-term mental health effects of childhood play experience', *Children's Geographies*, vol 5, no 3, pp 283-96.

Blom, B. and Morén, S. (2010) 'Explaining social work practice – the CAIMeR theory', *Journal of Social Work*, vol 10, no 1, pp 98-119.

Bloor, M. (1997) 'Addressing social problems through qualitative research', in D. Silverman (ed) *Qualitative research: Theory, method and practice*, London: Sage Publications.

Bloor, M. (2010) 'Commentary: the researcher's obligation to bring about good', *Qualitative Social Work*, vol 9, no 1, pp 17-20.

Bloor, M. and McKeganey, N. (1989) 'Ethnography addressing the practitioner' in J. Gubrium and D. Silverman (eds) *The Politics of Field Research: Sociology Beyond Enlightenment*, Newbury Park, CA: Sage Publications.

Branco, F.J.N. (2016) 'The circle of social reform: the relationship social work-social policy in Addams and Richmond', *European Journal of Social Work*, vol 19, no 3-4, pp 405-19.

Brante, T. and Elzinga, A. (1990) 'Towards a theory of scientific controversies', *Science Studies*, no 2, pp 33-46.

Brekke, J. (2012) 'Shaping a science of social work', *Research on Social Work Practice*, no 22, pp 455-64.

Burawoy, M. (2005) 'For public sociology', *American Sociological Review*, vol 70, no 1, pp 4-28.

Burgess, E.W. (1916) 'The social survey a field for constructive service by departments of Sociology', *American Journal of Sociology*, vol 21, no 4, pp 492-500.

Burgess, E.W. (1928) 'What social case records should contain to be useful for sociological interpretation', *Social Forces*, vol 6, no 4, pp 524-32.

Burrow, J.W. (1970) *Evolution and society*, Cambridge: Cambridge University Press.

Campbell, D.T. (1964) 'Distinguishing differences of perception from failures of communication in cross-cultural studies', in F. Northrop and H. Livingston (eds) *Cross-cultural understanding: Epistemology in anthropology*, New York, NY: Harper & Row.

Campbell, D.T. (1978) 'Qualitative knowing in action research', in M. Brenner and P. Marsh (eds) *The social context of methods*, London: Croom Helm.

Campbell, D.T. (1979) 'Degrees of freedom and the case study', in T.D. Cook and C.S. Reichardt (eds) *Qualitative and quantitative methods in evaluation research*, Beverly Hills, CA: Sage Publications.

Campbell, D. T. (1981) 'Comment: another perspective on a scholarly career', in M.B. Brewer and B.E. Collins (eds) 'Perspectives on knowing: six themes from Donald T Campbell', *Scientific inquiry and the social sciences*, San Francisco, CA: Jossey Bass.

Campbell, D.T. (1994) 'Foreword', in R.K. Yin (ed) *Case study research*, Thousand Oaks, CA: Sage Publications.

Campbell, D.T. (1996) 'Can we overcome worldview incommensurability/relativity in trying to understand the other?', in R. Jessor, A. Colby and R. Shweder (eds) *Ethnography and human development*, Chicago, IL: University of Chicago Press.

Campbell, D. T and Russo, M.J. (1999) *Social experimentation*, Thousand Oaks, CA: Sage Publications.

Carey, M. (2014) 'Mind the gaps: understanding the rise and implications of different types of cynicism in statutory social work', *British Journal of Social Work*, vol 44, no 1, pp 127-44.

Carroll, L. (1893) *Sylvia and Bruno concluded*, London: Macmillan and Co.

Cefaï, D. (2015) 'Outreach work in Paris: a moral ethnography of social work and nursing with homeless people', *Human Studies*, no 38, pp 137-56.

Chambon, A. (2008) 'Social work and the arts: Critical imagination', in J.G. Knowles and A. Cole (eds) *Handbook of the arts in qualitative research: Perspectives, methodologies, examples*, Thousand Oaks, CA: Sage Publications.

Chambon, A. (2012) 'Disciplinary borders and borrowings: social work knowledge and its social reach: a historical perspective', *Social Work and Society*, vol 10, no 2, www.socwork.net/sws/article/view/348.

Chapin, F.S. (1932) 'The advantages of experimental sociology in the study of family group patterns', *Social Forces*, no 11, pp 200-7.

Chapin, F.S. (1955 [1947]) *Experimental designs in sociological research*, New York, NY: Harper.

Chapin, F.S. and Queen, S.A. (1972 [1937]) *Research memorandum on social work in the Depression*, Social Science Research Council, Bulletin No 39, New York, NY: Arno Press.

Clark, A. and Emmel, N. (2010) 'Using walking interviews', Realities Toolkit #13, Morgan Centre for the Study of Relationships and Personal Life, University of Manchester, www.socialsciences. manchester.ac.uk/morgan-centre/research/resources/toolkits/ toolkit-13/.

Collins, H. and Pinch, T. (1998) *The Golem at large: What you should know about technology*, Cambridge: Cambridge University Press.

Comstock, D. (1982) 'A method for critical research', in F. Bredo and W. Feinburg (eds) *Knowledge and values in educational research*, Philadelphia, PA: Temple University Press.

Cronbach, L. (1982) *Designing evaluations of educational and social programs*, San Francisco, CA: Jossey-Bass.

Cronbach, L. (1986) 'Social inquiry by and for Earthlings', in D.W. Fiske and R.A. Shweder (eds) *Metatheory in social science*, Chicago, IL: University of Chicago.

Cronbach, L., Ambron, S., Dornbusch, S., Hess, R., Hornik, R., Phillips, D., Walker, D. and Weiner, S. (1980) *Toward reform of program evaluation*, San Francisco, CA: Jossey-Bass.

Cummings, J.N. and Kiesler, S. (2005) 'Collaborative research across disciplinary and organizational boundaries', *Social Studies of Science*, vol 35, no 5, pp 703-22.

Davies, M. (2013) 'Maintenance theory', in M. Davies (ed) *The Blackwell companion to social work*, Oxford: Wiley-Blackwell.

de Montigny, G. (Forthcoming) 'Social workers' peculiar contribution to ethnographic research', *Qualitative Social Work*, DOI: 10.1177/1473325016678310 .

Denzin, N.K. (2002) 'Social work in the seventh moment', *Qualitative Social Work*, vol 1, no 1, pp 25-38.

Dimitriadis, G. (2006) 'The situation complex: revisiting Frederic Thrasher's *The gang: A study of 1,313 gangs in Chicago*', *Cultural Studies Critical Methodologies*, vol 6, no 3, pp 335-52.

Dominelli, L. (2010) 'Globalization, contemporary challenges and social work practice', *International Social Work*, vol 53, no 5, pp 599-612.

Dunk-West, P. and Verity, F. (2013) *Sociological social work*, Farnham: Ashgate Publishing.

Edwards, A., Barnes, M., Plewis, I. and Morris, K. (2006) *Working to prevent the social exclusion of children and young people: Final lessons from the national evaluation of the Children's Fund*, DfES Research Report 734, London: DfES.

England, H. (1986) *Social work as art*, London: Allen and Unwin.

Erickson, M. (2002) 'Science as a vocation in the 21st century: an empirical study of science researchers', *Max Weber Studies*, vol 3, no 1, pp 33-55.

Evans, T. (2011) 'Professionals, managers and discretion: critiquing street-level bureaucracy', *British Journal of Social Work*, vol 41, no 2, pp 368-86.

Evans, T. (2016) 'Street-level bureaucracy, management and the corrupted world of service', *European Journal of Social Work,* vol 19, no 5, pp 602-615.

Evans, T. and Harris, J. (2004) 'Street level bureaucracy, social work and the (exaggerated) death of discretion', *British Journal of Social Work*, vol 34, no 6, pp 871-95.

Faris, R.E.L. (1967) *Chicago sociology (1920-1932)*, San Francisco, CA: Chandler Publishing Co.

Flick, U. (2006) *An introduction to qualitative research*, London: Sage Publications.

Flick, U. and Röhnsch, G. (2007) 'Idealization and neglect: health concepts of homeless adolescents', *Journal of Health Psychology*, vol 12, no 5, pp 737-49.

Fortune, A.E. (2012) 'Development of the task-centered model', in T.L. Rzepnicki, S.G. McCracken and H.E. Briggs (eds) *From task-centered social work to evidence-based and integrative practice: Reflections on history and implementation*, Chicago, IL: Lyceum Books.

Fortune, A.E. (2014) 'How quickly we forget: comments on "A historical analysis of evidence-based practice in social work: the unfinished journey towards an empirically grounded profession"', *Social Service Review*, vol 88, no 2, pp 217-23.

Foucault, M. (1991a) 'What is an author?', in P. Rabinow (ed) *The Foucault reader*, London: Penguin Books.

Foucault, M. (1991b) 'Questions of method', in G. Burchell, C. Gordon and P. Miller (eds) *The Foucault effect*, Chicago, IL: University of Chicago Press, pp 73-86.

Fulford, B. and Columbo, A. (2004) 'Six models of mental disorder: a study combining linguistic analysis and empirical methods', *Journal of Philosophy, Psychiatry and Psychology*, vol 11, no 4, pp 129-44.

Fuller, S. (2006) *The new sociological imagination*, London: Sage Publications.

Fuller, S. (2009) *The sociology of intellectual life*, London: Sage Publications.

Gal, J. and Weiss-Gal, I. (2017) *Where academia and policy meet*, Bristol: Policy Press.

Giddens, A. (1993) *New rules of sociological method*, Stanford, CA: Stanford University Press.

Gomory, T. (2001) 'A fallibilistic response to Thyer's theory of theory-free empirical research in social work practice', *Journal of Social Work Education*, vol 37, no 1, pp 26-50.

Gould, N. and Baldwin, M. (eds) (2004) *Social work, critical reflection and the learning organization*, Aldershot: Ashgate.

Greenspan, N.T. (2005) *The end of the certain world*, Chichester, UK: John Wiley and Sons.

Greenwood, E. (1945) *Experimental sociology: A study in method*, New York, NY: Farrar, Strauss and Giroux.

Grisso, T. and Vincent, G.M. (2005) 'The empirical limits of forensic mental health assessment', *Law and Human Behavior*, vol 29, no 1, pp 1-5.

Gross, M. (2010) '"All life is experimentation": the Chicago School and the experimenting society', in C. Hart (ed) *The legacy of the Chicago School*, Poynton: Midrash Publications, pp 174-84.

Grossberg, L. (1996) 'On postmodernism and articulation: an interview with Stuart Hall', in D. Morley and K.H. Chen (eds) *Stuart Hall: Critical dialogues in cultural studies*, London: Routledge.

Gubrium, J.F. (2016) 'From the iron cage to everyday life', in J.F. Gubrium, T.A. Andreassen, and P.K. Solvang (eds) *Reimagining the human service relationship*, New York, NY: Columbia University Press.

Gubrium, J.F., Andreassen, T.A. and Solvang, P.K. (eds) (2016) *Reimagining the human service relationship*, New York, NY: Columbia University Press.

Hackett, E.J. (2005) 'Introduction. Special guest issue on scientific collaboration', *Social Studies of Science*, vol 35, no 5, pp 667-71.

Hall, T., Lashua, B. and Coffey, A. (2008) 'Sound and the everyday in qualitative research', *Qualitative Inquiry*, vol 14, no 6, pp 1019-40.

Halmos, P. (1965) *The faith of the counsellors*, London: Constable and Company.

Halmos, P. (1970) *The personal service society*, London: Constable and Company.

Hammersley, M. (1995) *The politics of social research*, London: Sage Publications.

Hammersley, M. (2000) 'The relevance of qualitative research', *Oxford Review of Education*, vol 26, no 3/4, pp 393-405.

Harré, R. (1989) 'Language games and texts of identity', in J. Shotter and K. Gergen (eds) *Texts of identity*, Newbury Park: Sage.

Heidegger, M. (1971) 'The thing', in *Poetry, language, thought*, trans. Albert Hofstadter, New York, NY: Harper & Row, pp 163-86.

Helm, P. (1987) 'Why be objective?', in P. Helm (ed) (1987) *Objective knowledge: A Christian perspective*, Leicester: Inter-varsity Press, pp 29-40.

Hill, A. and Shaw, I. (2011) *Social work and ICT*, London: Sage Publications.

Hitchings, H. (2008) *The secret life of words: How English became English*, London: John Murray.

Hodgetts, D., Radley, A., Chamberlain, K and Hodgetts, A. (2007) 'Health inequalities and homelessness: considering material, spatial and relational dimensions', *Journal of Health Psychology*, vol 12, no 5, pp 709-25.

Høgsbro, K. and Shaw, I. (eds) (2017) *Social work and research in advanced welfare states*, London: Taylor and Francis.

Holesko, M. and Thyer, B. (2011) *Pocket glossary of commonly used research terms*, Thousand Oaks, CA: Sage Publications.

Holland, S., Burgess, S., Grogan-Kaylor, A. and Delva, J. (2011) 'Understanding neighbourhoods, communities and environments: new approaches for social work research', *British Journal of Social Work*, vol 41, no 4, pp 689-707.

Holman, B. (1987) 'Research from the underside', *British Journal of Social Work*, vol 17, no 6, pp 669-83.

Holstein, J.A. and Gubrium, J.F. (1995) *The active interview*, Thousand Oaks, CA: Sage Publications.

Hong, P.Y. and Song, I.H. (2010) 'Glocalization of social work practice: global and local responses to globalization', *International Social Work*, vol 53, no 5, pp 656-70.

Hooykaas, R. (1972) *Religion and the rise of modern science*, Edinburgh: Scottish Academic Press.

Horkheimer, M. (2002) *Critical theory: Selected essays*, New York, NY: Continuum.

House, E. (1980) *Evaluating with validity*, Beverly Hills, CA: Sage Publications.

House, E. (1991a) 'Evaluation and social justice: where are we now?', in M. McLaughlin and D. Phillips (eds) *Evaluation and education: At quarter century*, Chicago, IL: Chicago University Press.

House, E. (1991b) 'Realism in research', *Educational Researcher*, vol 20, no 6, pp 2-9.

House, E. (1993) *Professional evaluation*, Newbury Park, CA: Sage Publications.

House, E. (1995) 'Putting things together coherently: logic and justice', in D. Fournier (ed) *Reasoning in evaluation: Inferential links and leaps*, San Francisco, CA: American Evaluation Association/Jossey-Bass.

IFSW/IASSW (International Federation of Social Workers/International Association of Schools of Social Work) (2007) *International definition of the social work profession*, Supplement of *International Social Work*, London: Sage Publications.

Jacob, M.C. (1992) 'Science and politics in the late twentieth century', *Social Research*, vol 59, no 3, pp 487-503.

Jerrim, J. and de Vries, R. (2017) 'The limitations of quantitative social science for informing public policy', *Evidence & Policy*, vol 13, no 1, pp 117-33.

Kemp, S. (2012) 'Evaluating interests in social science: beyond objectivist evaluation and the non-judgemental stance', *Sociology*, vol 46, no 4, pp 664-79.

Kirk, S. and Reid, W.J. (2002) *Science and social work*, New York, NY: Columbia University Press.

Kuhn, T.S. (1970) *The structure of scientific revolutions*, Chicago, IL: Chicago University Press.

Latour, B. (1992) 'One more turn after the social turn: easing science studies into the non-modern world', in E. McMullin (ed) *The social dimensions of science*, Notre Dame, IN: Notre Dame University Press, pp 272-92.

Lee, R. (forthcoming) 'Interviewing, social work and Chicago sociology in the 1920s', *Qualitative Social Work*.

Lees, A. (ed) (2004) *Character is destiny: The autobiography of Alice Salomon*, Ann Arbor, MI: University of Michigan Press.

Lee, R. (2008) 'David Riesman and the sociology of the interview', *The Sociological Quarterly*, vol 49, no 2, pp 285-307.

Lengermann, P. and Niebrugge, G. (2007) 'Thrice told: narratives of sociology's relation to social work', in C. Calhoun (ed) *Sociology in America: A history*, Chicago, IL: University of Chicago Press, pp 63-114.

Lengermann, P.M. and Niebrugge-Brantley, J. (2002) 'Back to the future: settlement sociology 1885-1930', *The American Sociologist*, vol 33, no 3, pp 5-20.

Lunt, N., Fouché, C. and Yates, D. (2008) *Growing research in practice: Report of an innovative partnership model*, Wellington: Families Commission.

Lunt, N., Ramian, K., Shaw, I., Mitchell, F. and Fouché, C. (2012) 'Networking practitioner research: the state of the art', *European Journal of Social Work*, vol 15, no 2, pp 185-203.

Lyon, D. (2001) *Surveillance society: Monitoring everyday life*, Buckingham: Open University Press.

Lyon, D. (2007) *Surveillance studies: An overview*, Cambridge: Polity Press.

Lyon, D. and Bauman, Z. (2013) *Liquid surveillance: A conversation*, Cambridge: Polity Press.

Macdonald, G. and Popay, J. (2010) 'Evidence and practice: the knowledge challenge for social work', in I. Shaw, K. Briar-Lawson, J. Orme and R. Ruckdeschel (eds) *Sage handbook of social work research*, London: Sage Publications.

MacIver, R.M. (1931) *The contribution of sociology to social Work*, New York, NY: Columbia University Press.

MacKay, D. (1987) 'Objectivity as a Christian value', in P. Helm (ed) *Objective knowledge: A Christian perspective*, Leicester: Inter-varsity Press.

MacKay, D. (1979) *Human science and human dignity*, London: Hodder and Stoughton.

Madge, J. (1953) *The tools social science*, London: Longmans Green and Co.

Mafile'o, T. (2004) 'Exploring Tongan social work: *Fakafekau'aki* (connecting) and *Fakatokilalo* (humility)', *Qualitative Social Work*, vol 3, no 3, pp 239-57.

Mandell, N. (1988) 'The least adult role in studying children', *Journal of Contemporary Ethnography*, vol 16, no 4, pp 433-67.

Markham, A. and Buchanan, E. (2012) 'Ethical decision-making and internet research: recommendations from the AoIR Ethics Working Committee (Version 2.0), http://aoir.org/reports/ethics2.pdf.

Martin, M. (2007) 'Crossing the line: observations from East Detroit, Michigan USA', *Qualitative Social Work*, vol 6, no 4, pp 465-75.

Martindale, D. (1961) *The nature and types of sociological theory*, London: Routledge and Kegan Paul.

Massey, D. (1991) 'A global sense of place', *Marxism Today*, June, pp 24-29.

McEwan, I. (1998) *Amsterdam*, London: Vintage Books.

McGuinness, P. (2015) *Other people's countries*, London: Vintage Books.

McGuire, J. (ed) (1995) *What works? Reducing reoffending*, London: Wiley.

McMahon, A. (1998) *Damned if you do, damned if You don't*, Aldershot: Ashgate.

Medawar, P. (1984) *The limits of science*, Oxford: Oxford University Press.

Merton, R.K. (1971) 'Social problems and sociological theory', in R. Merton and R. Nisbet (eds) *Contemporary social problems*, New York, NY: Harcourt Brace Jovanovich, Inc.

Merton, R.K. and Barber, E. (2004) *The travels and adventures of serendipity*, Princeton, NJ: Princeton University Press.

Milligan, C. (2001) *Geographies of care: Space, place and the voluntary sector*, Aldershot: Ashgate.

Milligan, C. and Fife, N. (2004) 'Putting the voluntary sector in its place: geographical perspectives on voluntary activity and social welfare in Glasgow', *Journal of Social Policy*, vol 33, no 1, pp 73-93.

Milligan, C., Gatrell, A.C. and Bingley, A. (2004) 'Cultivating health: therapeutic landscapes and older people in Northern England', *Social Science and Medicine*, vol 58, no 9, pp 1781-93.

Mills, C.W. (1943) 'The professional ideology of social pathologists', *American Journal of Sociology*, vol 49, no 2, pp 165-80.

Mills, C.W. (1970) *The sociological imagination*, Harmondsworth: Penguin Books.

Mitchell, F., Lunt, N. and Shaw I. (2010) 'Practitioner research in social work: a knowledge review', *Evidence & Policy*, vol 6, no 1, pp 7-31.

Mullen, E.J. (2016) 'Reconsidering the idea of "evidence" in evidence-based policy and practice', *European Journal of Social Work*, vol 19, no 3-4, pp 310-35.

Murdach, A. (2007) 'Situational approaches to direct practice. Origin, decline and re-Emergence', *Social Work*, vol 52, no 3, pp 211-18.

Neander, K and Skott, C. (2006) 'Important meetings with important persons: narratives from families facing adversity and their key figures', *Qualitative Social Work*, vol 5, no 3, pp 295-311.

Nind, M. (2015) 'What is innovative in research methods?', Paper for National Centre for Research Methods, http://slideplayer.com/slide/4485683.

Nowotny, H. (2003) 'Dilemma of expertise: democratising expertise and socially robust knowledge', *Science and Public Policy*, vol 30, no 3, pp 151-6.

Oakley, A. (1999) 'Paradigm wars: some thoughts on a personal and public trajectory', *International Journal of Social Research Methodology*, vol 2, no 3, pp 247-54.

Oakley, A. (2014) *Father and daughter: Patriarchy, gender and social science*, Bristol: Policy Press.

Oancea, A. and Furlong, J. (2007) 'Expressions of excellence and the assessment of applied and practice-based research', *Research Papers in Education*, vol 22, no 2, pp 119-37.

O'Farrell, C. (2005) *Michel Foucault*, London: Sage Publications.

Okpych, N.J. and Yu, J.L.-H. (2014) 'A historical analysis of evidence-based practice in social work: the unfinished journey toward an empirically grounded profession', *Social Service Review*, vol 88, no 1, pp 3-58.

Orme, J. and Briar-Lawson, K. (2010) 'Theory and knowledge about social problems to enhance policy development', in I. Shaw, K. Briar-Lawson, J. Orme and R. Ruckdeschel (eds) *Sage handbook of social work research*, London: Sage Publications.

Packer, M. (2011) *The science of qualitative research*, Cambridge: Cambridge University Press.

Park, R.E. (1924) 'The significance of social research in social service', *Journal of Applied Sociology*, May-June, pp 263-7.

Parton, N. (2007) 'Constructive social work practice in an age of uncertainty', in S.L. Witkin and D. Saleelbey (eds) *Social work dialogues: Transforming the canon in inquiry, practice and education*, Alexandra, VA: Council on Social Work Education.

Parton, N. (2008a) 'Towards the preventative-surveillance state: the current changes in children's services in England', in K. Burns and D. Lynch (eds) *Child protection and welfare social work: Contemporary themes and practice perspectives*, Dublin: A & A Farmar.

Parton, N. (2008b) 'Changes in the form of knowledge in social work: from the "social" to the "informational"?', *British Journal of Social Work*, vol 38, no 2, pp 253-69.

Parton, N. (2014) 'Social work, child protection and politics: some critical and constructive reflections', *British Journal of Social Work*, vol 44, pp 2042–56.

Parton, N. and Kirk, S. (2010) 'The nature and purposes of social work', in I. Shaw, K. Briar-Lawson, J. Orme and R. Ruckdeschel (eds) *Sage handbook of social work research*, London: Sage Publications.

Parton, N. and O'Byrne, P. (2000) *Constructive social work: Towards a new practice*, London: Macmillan.

Pease, B. (2010) 'Challenging the dominant paradigm: social work research, social justice and social change', I. Shaw, K. Briar-Lawson, J. Orme and R. Ruckdeschel (eds) *Sage handbook of social work research*, London: Sage Publications.

Phillips, D.C. (2000) *The expanded social scientist's bestiary*, Lanham, MA: Rowan and Littlefield.

Pithouse, A., Hall, C., Peckover, S. and White, S. (2009) 'A tale of two CAFs: the impact of the electronic Common Assessment Framework', *British Journal of Social Work*, vol 39, no 4, pp 599-612.

Platt, J. (1996) *A history of sociological research methods in America, 1920-1960*, Cambridge: Cambridge University Press.

Platt, J.R. (1964) 'Strong inference', *Science*, New Series, vol 146, no 3642, pp 347-53.

Polanyi, M. (1966) *The tacit dimension*, Chicago, IL: University of Chicago Press.

Popay, J., Thomas, C., Williams, G., Bennett, S., Gatrell, A. and Bostock, L. (2003) 'A proper place to live: health inequalities, agency and the normative dimensions of space', *Social Science and Medicine*, vol 57, no 1, pp 55-65.

Popkewitz, T. (1990) 'Whose future? Whose past?', in E. Guba (ed) *The paradigm dialog*, Newbury Park, CA: Sage Publications.

Popper, K. (1966) *The open society and its enemies, Volume 2*, London: Routledge and Kegan Paul.

Presidential Advice to Younger Sociologists (1953) *American Sociological Review*, vol 18, no 6, pp 597-604.

Queen, S.A. (1922) *Social work in the light of history*, Philadelphia, PA: Lippincott.

Ramian, K. (2004) 'Praktikere i praksisforskning' ('Practitioners in practice research'), in K. Høgsbro (ed) *Socialpsykiatriens kompleksitet*, Copenhagen: Samfundslitteratur.

Reckless, W.C. (1928) 'Suggestions for the sociological study of problem children', *Journal of Educational Sociology*, vol 2, no 3, pp 156-71.

Reckless, W.C. (1929) 'A sociological case study of a foster child', *Journal of Educational Sociology*, vol 2, no 10, pp 567-84.

Reid, W.J. (1988) 'Service effectiveness and the social agency', in R. Patti, J. Poertner and C. Rapp (eds) *Managing for effectiveness in social welfare organizations*, New York, NY: Haworth.

Reid, W.J. and Shyne, A.W. (1969) *Brief and extended casework*, New York, NY: Columbia University Press.

Riemann, G. (2005) 'Ethnographies of practice – practicing ethnography', *Journal of Social Work Practice*, vol 19, no 1, pp 87-101.

Riemann, G. (2011) 'Self-reflective ethnographies of practice and their relevance for professional socialisation in social work', *International Journal of Action Research,* vol 7, no 3, pp 262-93.

Robinson, R. (2016) *Every little sound*, Liverpool: Liverpool University Press.

Rodwell, M.K. (1998) *Social work constructivist research*, London: Routledge.

Romm, N. (1995) 'Knowing as an intervention', *Systems Practice*, vol 8, no 2, pp 137-67.

Romm, N. (1996) 'Inquiry-and-intervention in systems planning: probing methodological rationalities', *World Futures*, no 47, pp 25-36.

Rooney, R.H. (2010) 'Task-centered practice in the United States', in A. Fortune, P. McCallion and K. Briar-Lawson (eds) *Social work practice research for the 21st century*, New York, NY: Columbia University Press, pp 195-202.

Sackett, D., Rosenberg, W., Gray, J., Haynes, R. and Richardson, W. (1996) 'Evidence-based medicine: What it is and what it isn't', *British Medical Journal*, vol 312, no 7023, pp 71-72.

Schirmer, W. and Michailakis, D. (2015a) 'The Luhmannian approach to exclusion/inclusion and its relevance to social work', *Journal of Social Work*, vol 15, no 1, pp 45-64.

Schirmer, W. and Michailakis, D. (2015b) 'The help system and its reflection theory: a sociological observation of social work', *Nordic Social Work Research*, no 5, suppl 1, pp 71-84.

Schirmer, W. and Michailakis, D. (2016) 'Inclusion/exclusion as the missing link: a Luhmannian analysis of loneliness among older people', *Systems Research and Behavioral Science*, Wiley Online Library, DOI: 10.1002/sres.2441.

Schivelbusch, W. (1977) *The railway journey: The industrialization of time and space in the 19th century*, Los Angeles, CA: University of California Press.

Schön, D. (1992) 'The crisis of professional knowledge and the pursuit of an epistemology of practice', *Journal of Interprofessional Care*, vol 6, no 1, pp 49-63.

Schön, D. (1983) *The reflective practitioner: How professionals think in action*, New York, NY: Basic Books.

Schwab, J. (1969) 'The practical: a language for curriculum', *School Review*, November, pp 1-23.

Schwandt, T. (1993) 'Theory for the moral sciences: crisis of identity and purpose', in D. Flinders and G. Mills (eds) *Theory and concepts in qualitative research: Perspectives from the field*, New York, NY: Teachers College Press.

Schwandt, T. (1997) 'Evaluation as practical hermeneutics', *Evaluation*, vol 3, no 1, pp 69-83.

Scott, D. (1990) 'Practice wisdom: the neglected source of practice research', *Social Work*, vol 35, no 6, pp 564-8.

Scriven, M. (1986) 'New frontiers of evaluation', *Evaluation Practice*, vol 7, no 1, pp 7-44.

Shadish, W., Cook, T. and Leviton, L. (1990) *Foundations of program evaluation: Theories of practice*, Newbury Park, CA: Sage Publications.

Shaw, I. (1999) *Qualitative evaluation*, London: Sage Publications.

Shaw, I. (2007) 'Is social work research distinctive?', *Social Work Education*, vol 26, no 7, pp 659-69.

Shaw, I. (2008) 'Ethics and the practice of qualitative research', *Qualitative Social Work*, vol 7, no 4, pp 400-14.

Shaw, I. (2009) 'Rereading *The Jack-Roller*: hidden histories in sociology and social work', *Qualitative Inquiry*, vol 15, no 7, pp 1241-64.

Shaw, I. (2011) 'Social work research – an urban desert?', *European Journal of Social Work*, vol 14, no 1, pp 11-26.

Shaw, I. (2012) 'The positive contributions of quantitative methodology to social work research: a view from the sidelines', *Research on Social Work Practice*, vol 22, no 2, pp 129-34.

Shaw, I. (2014a) 'A science of social work? Response to John Brekke', *Research on Social Work Practice*, vol 24, no 5, pp 524-26.

Shaw, I. (2014b) 'Sociology and social work: in praise of limestone?', in J. Holmwood and J. Scott (eds) *The Palgrave handbook of sociology in Britain*, London: Palgrave, pp 123-54.

Shaw, I. (2014c) 'Sociological social work: a cartoon', *European Journal of Social Work*, vol 17, no 5, pp 754-70.

Shaw, I. (2015a) 'The archaeology of research practices: a social work case', *Qualitative Inquiry*, vol 21, no 1, pp 36-49.

Shaw, I. (2015b) 'Sociological social workers: a history of the present?', *Nordic Journal of Social Work Research*, no 5, suppl 1, pp 7-24.

Shaw, I. (2106a) *Social work science*, New York, NY: Columbia University Press.

Shaw, I. (2016b) 'Case work: re-forming the relationship between sociology and social work', *Qualitative Research*, vol 16, no 1, pp 60-77.

Shaw, I. (forthcoming) '"Let us go then, you and I": journeying with Ada Eliot Sheffield', *Qualitative Social Work*, DOI: 10.1177/1473325017699454, first published 11 April 2017.

Shaw, I. and Holland, S. (2014) *Doing qualitative research in social work*, London: Sage Publications.

Shaw, I. and Lunt, N. (2011) 'Navigating practitioner research', *British Journal of Social Work*, vol 41, no 8, pp 1548-65.

Shaw, I. and Lunt, N. (2012) 'Constructing practitioner research', *Social Work Research*, vol 36, no 3, pp 197-208.

Shaw, I. and Lunt, N. (forthcoming) 'Forms of practitioner research', *British Journal of Social Work*, DOI: 10.1093/bjsw/bcx024, first published 17 April 2017.

Shaw, I. and Norton, M. (2007) *Kinds and quality of social work research in higher education*, London: Social Care Institute for Excellence, www.scie.org.uk/publications/reports/report17.asp.

Shaw, I. and Norton, M. (2008) 'Kinds and quality of social work research', *British Journal of Social Work*, vol 38, no 5, pp 953-70.

Shaw, I. and Shaw, A. (1997) 'Game plans, buzzes and sheer luck: doing well in social work', *Social Work Research*, vol 21, no 2, pp 69-79. Reprinted in S. Kirk (ed) (1999) *Social work research methods: Building knowledge for practice*, Washington, DC: NASW Press.

Shaw, I., Briar-Lawson, K., Orme, J. and Ruckdeschel, R. (2010) 'Mapping social work research: pasts, presents and futures', in I. Shaw, K. Briar-Lawson, J. Orme and R. Ruckdeschel (eds) *Sage handbook of social work research*, London: Sage Publications.

Shaw, I., Lunt, N. and Mitchell, F. (2014) *Practitioner Research and Social Care: a Review and Recommendations*, Methods Review 18, London: NIHR School for Social Care Research.

Shaw, I., Hardy, M. and Marsh, J. (eds) (2016) *Social work research*, London: Sage Publications.

Sheffield, A. E. (1920) *The social case history: Its construction and content*, New York, NY: Russell Sage Foundation.

Sheffield, A.E. (1922) *Case-study possibilities, a forecast*, Boston, MA: Research Bureau on Social Case Work.

Sheffield, A.E. (1937) *Social insight in case situations*, New York, NY: Appleton-Century Company.

Siporin, M. (1972) 'Situational assessment and intervention', *Social Casework*, vol 53, no 2, pp 91-109.

Siporin, M. (1975) *Introduction to social work practice*, New York, NY: Macmillan Publishing.

Smale, G., Tuson, G. and Statham, D. (2000) *Social work and social problems*, London: Macmillan.

Small, A. (1921) 'The future of sociology', *Publications of the American Sociological Society*, no 16, pp 174-93.

Small, A.W. (1903) 'What is a sociologist?', *American Journal of Sociology*, no 8, pp 468-77.

Specht, H. and Courtney, M. (1994) *Fallen angels: How social work has abandoned its mission*, New York, NY: Free Press.

Spong, S. (2007) 'Scepticism and belief: unravelling the relationship between theory and practice in counselling and psychotherapy', in S.R. Smith (ed) *Applying theory to policy and practice: Issues for critical reflection*, Aldershot: Ashgate.

Stake, R.E. and Schwandt, T.A. (2006) 'On discerning quality in evaluation', in I. Shaw, J. Greene and M. Mark, M. (eds) *Sage handbook of evaluation*, London: Sage Publications.

Staller, K. (2010) 'Technology and inquiry: past, present and future', *Qualitative Social Work*, vol 9, no 2, pp 285-87.

Stokes, D. E. (1997) *Pasteur's Quadrant: Basic science and technological innovation*, Washington DC: Brookings Institution.

Thomas, R.S. (1986) *Selected poems 1946-1968*, Newcastle upon Tyne: Bloodaxe Books.

Thrasher, F.M. (1927) *The gang: A study of 1,313 gangs in Chicago*, Chicago, IL: University of Chicago Press.

Thrasher, F.M. (1928a) 'The study of the total situation', *Journal of Educational Sociology*, vol 1, no 10, pp 599-612.

Thrasher, F.M. (1928b) 'How to study the boys' gang in the open', *Journal of Educational Sociology*, vol 1, no 5, pp 244-54.

Thyer, B.A. (ed) (2009) *Handbook of social research methods*, Thousand Oaks, CA: Sage Publications.

Timms, N. (1968) *The language of social casework*, London: Routledge and Kegan Paul.

Timms, N. (1972) '… and Renoir and Matisse and …', Inaugural Lecture, Bradford: University of Bradford.

Timms, N. (2014 [1967]) *A sociological approach to social problems*, London: Routledge and Kegan Paul.

Trevillion, S. (2010) 'From social work practice to social work research: an emergent approach to a basic problem', in I. Shaw, K. Briar-Lawson, J. Orme and R. Ruckdeschel (eds), *Sage handbook of social work research*, London: Sage Publications.

Trygged, S. (2010) 'Balancing the global and the local: some normative reflections on international social work', *International Social Work*, vol 53, no 5, pp 644-55.

Turner, S. (1996) 'The Pittsburgh Survey and the survey movement', in M.W. Greenwald and M. Anderson (eds) *Pittsburgh surveyed: Social science and social reform in the early twentieth century*, Pittsburgh, PA: University of Pittsburgh Press, pp 35-49.

Verd, J.M. and Porcel, S. (2012) 'An application of qualitative geographic information systems (GIS) in the field of urban sociology using ATLAS.ti: Uses and reflections', *Forum Qualitative Sozialforschung /Forum: Qualitative Social Research*, [S.l.], vol 13, no 2: www. qualitative-research.net/index.php/fqs/article/view/1847/3373.

Videka, L. and Blackburn, J.A. (2010) 'The intellectual legacy of William J Reid', in A. Fortune, P. McCallion and K. Briar-Lawson (eds) *Social work practice research for the 21st century*, New York, NY: Columbia University Press, pp 183-94.

Walton, R.G. (1982) *Social work 2000: The future of social work in a changing society*, London: Longman.

Weber, M. (1948 [1919]) 'Science as a vocation', in H.H. Gerth and C.W. Mills (eds) *From Max Weber: Essays in sociology*, London: Routledge and Kegan Paul, pp 129-56.

Webb, S.A. (2006) *Social work in a risk society*, London: Palgrave Macmillan.

Wiles, R., Pain, H. and Crow, G. (2009) *Innovation in qualitative research methods: a narrative review*, Swindon: ESRC Research Centre for Research Methods, http://eprints.ncrm.ac.uk/919/1/innovation_ in_qualitative_research_methods.pdf.

Williams, A. (ed) (2007) *Therapeutic landscapes*, Aldershot: Ashgate.

Williams, R. (1983) *Keywords: A vocabulary of culture and society*, London: Fontana Press.

Williamson, H. (2004) *Milltown boys revisited*, Oxford: Berg.

Witkin, S. (1999) 'Constructing our future', *Social Work*, vol 44, no 1, pp 5-8.

Witkin, S. (2017) *Transforming social work: Social constructionist reflections on contemporary and enduring issues*, New York, NY: Palgrave Macmillan.

Wolpert, L. and Richards, A. (1997) *Passionate minds: The inner world of scientists*, Oxford: Oxford University Press.

Woolgar, S. (1981) 'Interests and explanation in the social study of science', *Social Studies of Science*, no 11, pp 365-94.

Xenitidou, M. and Gilbert, N. (2009) *Innovations in social science research methods*, Guildford: University of Surrey, http://eprints.ncrm. ac.uk/919/1/innovation_in_qualitative_research_methods.pdf.

Young, E.F. (1925) 'The social base map', *Journal of Applied Sociology*, Jan-Feb, pp 202-6.

Young, P. (1928) 'Should case records be written in the first person?' *The Family*, vol 11, no 5, pp 153-54.

Young, P. (1928/1929) 'Sociological concepts as an aid to social work analysis', *Social Forces*, no 7, pp 497-500.

Young, P. (1929) 'A life history', Luther Bernard Papers, Pennsylvania State University.

Young, P. (1935) *Interviewing in social work: A sociological analysis*, New York, NY: McGraw Hill.

Young, P. and Young, E.F. (1928) 'Getting at the boy himself: through the personal interview', *Social Forces*, no 6, pp 408-15.

Index